WAVING GOODBYE
TO BABYLON

A call to look up and come out

Robert J Emery

Are the things you are living for worth Christ dying for?

LEONARD RAVENHILL

CONTENTS

INTRODUCTION

In times past, one of the greatest empires to have ever existed was the Chaldean empire with its capital city, Babylon. This nation features quite prominently in the Old Testament. However, in the New Testament, Babylon represents false religion. That is anything that has an appearance of godliness but fails to produce divine life that can only come from above.

In our lives, we often hold to practices that are, in fact, detestable in the sight of God. But we in our sinfulness use our religion to justify what is very clearly wrong. Instead of facing the music and bringing our idols into the light so God can deal with them, we cling to them and make excuses for our lack of obedience to the voice of God.

Yet God is calling unto Himself a people delivered from spiritual Babylon who has their sole affections not on this world but on the heavenly city, the world to come. Now is not the time for us to get comfortable down here. God is raising up a testimony for a lost world. A holy nation called out from the world set apart only for God. We are that nation, we are those people, and this is our time.

Everything we do must be for the Kingdom of God. So many Christians these days are stuck in Babylon trying to live a 'normal' life. Yet we are not called to be normal. We are a supernatural people and to live at ease while Zion burns is a terrible crime. Let us leave it all behind us as we follow Jesus Christ.

And I heard another voice from heaven saying, "Come out of her, my people, lest you share in her sins, and lest you receive of her plagues. - *Revelation 18:4*

CHAPTER ONE:
BABYLON – MORE
THAN A CITY

Babylon is the most featured city of the Bible; notably after Jerusalem, and was actually the capital of the neo-Babylonian (or Chaldean) empire. This city was the home of the infamous Nebuchadnezzar and many Israelites were exiled to Babylon as a result of their unfaithfulness to God.

By the rivers of Babylon,
There we sat down and wept,
When we remembered Zion.

> *- Psalm 137:1*

God scattered His people among the nations – one of which at this time was Babylonia, a place that God had stated that they would spend quite a bit of time. Yet God in His faithfulness to His covenant with the Patriarchs promised to bring them out of captivity into their own land.

"For thus says the Lord, 'When seventy years have been completed for Babylon, I will visit you and fulfill My good word to you, to bring you back to this place. For I know the plans that I have for you,' declares the Lord, 'plans for welfare and not for calamity to give you a future and a hope. Then you will call upon

Me and come and pray to Me, and I will listen to you. You will seek Me and find Me when you search for Me with all your heart.

- Jeremiah 29:10-13

It is fascinating that although God was very hard on the Jews in the way the Chaldeans handled them, there was such a remarkable promise of hope and future prosperity even amid such tragic darkness in Israel's history.

However, when the opportunity came for God to bring about His promise of restoration, many of the Jews living in Babylon had become very comfortable. Many of them were very successful and prosperous where they were driven (*See Deuteronomy 8:18 – this also explains why the Jews are good with money!*) They were called to be a separate people, but their values had started to intermix with the society around them.

Now when these things had been completed, the princes approached me, saying, "The people of Israel and the priests and the Levites have not separated themselves from the peoples of the lands, according to their abominations, those of the Canaanites, the Hittites, the Perizzites, the Jebusites, the Ammonites, the Moabites, the Egyptians and the Amorites. For they have taken some of their daughters as wives for themselves and for their sons, **so that the holy race has intermingled with the peoples of the lands; indeed, the hands of the princes and the rulers have been foremost in this unfaithfulness."**

- Ezra 9:1-2 (Emphasis added)

God called Israel to be a separate people, a nation called out from the rest of the world and separate unto Him. Yet despite this incredible call on their lives, the Israelites didn't really want to be so different from everyone else.

Nevertheless, the people refused to listen to the voice of Samuel, and they said, "No, but there shall be a king over us, **that we also may be like all the nations,** *that our king may judge us and go out before us and fight our battles."*

- 1 Samuel 8:19-20 (Emphasis added)

You see, to remain where they were in Babylon meant calamity for them. The judgement of God was fully set against Babylon. Her time was short; the writing was already on the wall, in a manner of speaking. To remain in Sodom was to be swept away in God's wrath with her. God warned His people:

Flee from the midst of Babylon, and each of you save his life Do not be destroyed in her punishment, for this is the Lord's time of vengeance; He is going to render recompense to her.

- Jeremiah 51:6

After this He says further on in the same passage:

Come forth from her midst, My people, and each of you save yourselves from the fierce anger of the Lord. *"Now so that your heart does not grow faint, and you are not afraid at the report that will be heard in the land—for the report will come one year, and after that another report in another year, and violence will be in the land with ruler against ruler—therefore behold, days are coming when I will punish the idols of Babylon; and her whole land will be put to shame and all her slain will fall in her midst.*

- Jeremiah 51:45-47 (Emphasis added)

In the same way, Christians have been saved and redeemed by the death and resurrection of the Lord and Saviour Jesus Christ. They have been set apart to be a people unique unto God alone. Yet many are fraternizing with the world and its idols. God is saying in 2 Corinthians 6:17:

""Therefore, come out from their midst and be separate," **says the Lord. "And do not touch what is unclean; and I** **will welcome you."**

11

A day is coming soon when God's mercy in delaying the day of judgment will come to an end. When that day does come, God will bring down His judgements on the world.

Of course, some will say 'Jesus is the friend of sinners,' to which the following can give an appropriate answer:

> The Pharisees and their scribes began grumbling at His disciples, saying, "Why do you eat and drink with the tax collectors and sinners?" And Jesus answered and said to them, "It is not those who are well who need a physician, but those who are sick. **I have not come to call the righteous but sinners to repentance.**"
>
> *- Luke 5:30-32 (Emphasis added)*

By eating and drinking with them, Jesus was calling these sinners out of their lifestyle of wretchedness. He most certainly was not eating and drinking and getting drunk, as some see it as their right to do so because of this. Howbeit it is worth noting that Jesus never calls Himself the friend of sinners and nor do any of the other New Testament writers. Instead, it was an insult given to Jesus by His enemies (*See Matthew 11:19 & Luke 7:34*). There are some Christians who for some unknown reason, unknown to the Bible and to God, who think that they have the freedom to flirt with the world.

> You adulteresses, do you not know that friendship with the world is hostility toward God? Therefore whoever wishes to be a friend of the world makes himself an enemy of God.
>
> *- James 4:4*

The Christian is in the world, but he or she is not of the world. They have been called out because God has called them to be a higher breed of people. It must bring a great deal of pain to the Lord's heart when He saves His people from the power of darkness and sin only to see them time and time again ignore Him while going off to play games with Babylon as if His death was for nothing. It is, of course, understandable and inevitable that falls and slips should happen. There is forgiveness and grace to cover the Christian who takes a tumble here or there.

In the New Testament, Babylon features prominently in Revelation as the final and complete expression of apostate and backslidden religion that embraces the world and is embraced by the world. However, it is finally going to be destroyed by God.

> *And another angel, a second one, followed, saying, "Fallen, fallen is Babylon the great, she who has made all the nations drink of the wine of the passion of her immorality."*
>
> *- Revelation 14:8*

The problem is not that in the future, this horrible world system will come into play under the antichrist. Folks; Babylon is alive and well today on planet earth. The same spirit that was creeping into the house of God in the day of Ezra is now creeping into churches today and ensnaring the minds of multitudes of God's own people.

Once, a group of Christians in my hearing were scolded for promiscuous behaviour during a prayer meeting. This telling off was not well received. They had a hard time listening to a rebuke directed at them. Why is it so hard for Christians to listen to correction? Why is it that, when confronted with the Word of God (regarding which Jesus said "Thy Word is truth" [John 17:17]), they frequently refuse to listen? They put it down to your opinion or something to do with the only culture, etc.

The answer is because the spirit of this age has crept into the Church, where Christians are no longer able to tell the difference between the holy and the profane. They want all the promises of God but none of the conditions or the commandments.

Yet God will deal with Babylon before the end comes; this is why the Church must separate herself from Babylon in these last days. The Church must be purely devoted to Jesus Christ alone. To obey His Word no matter what the cost is. There are many of God's people who are fully committed to Jesus Christ. May many more be added to the Church!

Why is the world so hard to let go?
It's all going to burn, didn't you know?
These are the things that dearly you held
My children, you're in love with the world

You speak great words when praising Me
But you forget all your works I can see
Hands held high to bring Me glory
But your life outside is another story

Stop your useless words of worthless lies
You think you are holy, but I see your disguise
How can you believe to be pure within?
When you love, embrace and hold onto sin?

Stop your games and all of your talk
You use your mouth, now walk the walk
How dare you go from adoring Me
To carnal things that fill you with glee

Repent now and stop being double minded
I know this is harsh, but you're being reminded
I saved you, to be a people separate unto Me
But you toy with the world, this is all I see

Please forsake this life and take up your cross
Stop strutting around like you're the boss
You are My beloved, but you cause a commotion
All because I am not your daily devotion

The pain you cause Me fills Me with tears
I have desired you for so many long years
Please don't leave Me alone again My wife
I gave my blood, I laid down My life

I long to be with you, even forever
I died a painful death to bring us together
I want to bring you close, and My heart uncover
But it's broken when you're with another

CHAPTER TWO: RIGHTS OR RESPONSIBILITIES?

Since this is the age of grace, one no longer belongs under the law. A most awesome and wonderful truth.

When you were dead in your transgressions and the uncircumcision of your flesh, He made you alive together with Him, having forgiven us all our transgressions, having canceled out the certificate of debt consisting of decrees against us, which was hostile to us; and He has taken it out of the way, having nailed it to the cross.

- Colossians 2:13-14

The Christian is no longer bound with the pomp and ceremony of keeping the law to approach God. There is such freedom when Christians allow Christ to enter their lives.

Now the Lord is the Spirit, and where the Spirit of the Lord is, there is liberty.

- 2 Corinthians 3:17

Liberty and joys are yours in the name of Jesus. Yet many do not really understand what this means. They neither understand the enormity of the wondrous freedoms they have nor the responsibilities these liberties entail.

For instance, there are some people, who mistakenly think that because they don't have to keep the law to be saved that God doesn't have standards that He expects His people to live by. Jesus didn't free you to sin but rather to free you from sin.

*She will bear a Son; and you shall call His name Jesus, **for He will save His people from their sins.***"

> *- Matthew 1:21 (Emphasis added)*

What then? Shall we sin because we are not under law but under grace? May it never be! Do you not know that when you present yourselves to someone as slaves for obedience, you are slaves of the one whom you obey, either of sin resulting in death, or of obedience resulting in righteousness? But thanks be to God that though you were slaves of sin, you became obedient from the heart to that form of teaching to which you were committed, and having been freed from sin, you became slaves of righteousness.

> *- Romans 6:15-18*

You are not free to sin; Jesus never came on this earth to die for your sins on the cross so that you could continue to live with them. He died and rose again to break the power of sin forever in your lives, and He expects you to follow after Him into a holy life. Jesus Christ demands it.

As obedient children, do not be conformed to the former lusts which were yours in your ignorance, but like the Holy One who called you, be holy yourselves also in all your behavior; because it is written, "You shall be holy, for I am holy."

> *- 1 Peter 1:14-16*

Now there is another area of this topic of freedom that must be addressed. So much of this freedom is spoken yet seldom ever do these same people ever consider the implications or the ramifications of such things that they affirm so strongly.

In the Bible, there is that famous passage about what Paul talks concerning matters of the conscience for which so many people love to quote to support their questionable idols. It is spoken so much about how what one person thinks is bad yet for another person this same thing can be okay, justifying love for this thing while not at all caring about or taking into consideration the feelings and opinions of the other person. To understand Paul's ideas, it is a necessity to consider the following passage of 1 Corinthians 8:

Now concerning things sacrificed to idols, we know that we all have knowledge. Knowledge makes arrogant, but love edifies. If anyone supposes that he knows anything, he has not yet known as he ought to know; but if anyone loves God, he is known by Him.

- 1 Corinthians 8:1-3

Paul is pointing out here exactly what was previously mentioned. Certain knowledge of our rights will puff us up, or make arrogant with no concern or care for the feelings of others. It is love for others that makes one want to edify them.

Therefore concerning the eating of things sacrificed to idols, we know that there is no such thing as an idol in the world, and that there is no God but one. For even if there are so-called gods whether in heaven or on earth, as indeed there are many gods and many lords, yet for us there is but one God, the Father, from whom are all things and we exist for Him; and one Lord, Jesus Christ, by whom are all things, and we exist through Him.

- 1 Corinthians 8:4-6

The issue at hand is one of eating food that has been offered to idols. In antiquity, meat was expensive and so poor people had a great deal of difficulty purchasing it, except at religious festivals where the food was undoubtedly sacrificed to a pagan god. Paul is saying here that the idols aren't anything. That is, there is only one true God, and these idols are just the dumb creation of people.

However not all men have this knowledge; but some, being accustomed to the idol until now, eat food as if it were sacrificed to an idol; and their conscience being weak is defiled. But food will not commend us to God; we are neither the worse if we do not eat, nor the better if we do eat. But take care that this liberty of yours does not somehow become a stumbling block to the weak. For if someone sees you, who have the knowledge, dining in an idol's temple, will not his conscience, if he is weak, be strengthened to eat things sacrificed to idols? For through your knowledge he who is weak is ruined, the brother for whose sake Christ died. **And so, by sinning against the brethren and wounding their conscience when it is weak, you sin against Christ. Therefore, if food causes my brother to stumble, I will never eat meat again, so that I will not cause my brother to stumble.**

- 1 Corinthians 8:7-13 (Emphasis added)

Paul is talking about our Christian freedom not being restricted to dietary laws (*however please do look at 1 Corinthians 10:20*) because certain Christians with stronger consciences felt free to eat such food they thought that they could do it willy-nilly. Whenever a brother or sister with a 'weaker' conscience would see them, they would be scandalised, and they would come under guilt should they try to exercise the same rights.

Paul is saying that to walk in a freedom that would offend another Christian or cause them to sin, is most certainly **not** loving. For Paul, he would instead give up meat altogether than to commit such a sin against a fellow believer. For him, it was absolutely unthinkable.

To help you understand this, there is a modern example of precisely this principle – one of the controversies of today. It regards tattoos, however before you roll your eyes, this is nothing at all about whether or not they are okay or about whether they are right or wrong but the attitude of some Christians. This is something of an altogether different kind of nature.

*'You shall not make any cuts in your body for the dead **nor make***

any tattoo marks on yourselves: I am the Lord.

- Leviticus 19:28 (Emphasis added)

There are arguments in favour for or against having tattoos. In the context of this verse, it seems that the tattoos here were done for the dead as a part of some cultic ritual. Those who would have tattoos immediately leap upon these cultural leanings as a way to embrace their rights as New Testament Christians, who have done away with trying to keep the law. Some of these (not all it must be added) Christians get angry when there are people who disagree with tattoos because after all, it is within their rights right? Remember what Paul said regarding his rights to eating meat? The same attitude of Paul displayed regarding meat should also be the attitude of the Christian who wishes to get tattoos. Rather than argue over what rights people have, they should have more concern over how they can love their neighbour as themselves and edify them. With Paul, one ought to say: *'I know I can within my rights have a tattoo. But since my Christian brothers and sisters disagree with me, I will scandalise them with getting one. So I will give up my right to have one to walk in love.'*

It is rare to find such a Christian. Actually having a tattoo in and of itself may not necessarily be wrong. Motivation is all important. Why do you want a tattoo? If you want a tattoo because the world promotes it, your friends have one, and you want to be fashionable before their eyes then let it be known to you: getting a tattoo **is** a sin for you. Christians should learn together how to walk in love and humility, putting the needs of the others above their own desires. Naturally, one finds this to be particularly difficult. All God wants is a for you to begin to take the steps towards Him. If you are willing to make the journey, God will give you the strength to live in the way that He wants you to.

Consider even this, in Scotland, Christians, don't drink. In Italy, everybody drinks a glass of wine with their meals. If the Christian from Italy came to Scotland and started drinking, they would scandalise the Church of Scotland! The loving thing for the Italian brother or sister to do is to refrain from any drinking in order not to offend the Scottish Christian. In the same way, if a Scot were to find himself in the home of the Italian believer and was offered a glass of wine, to refuse would offend the host. So in order not to offend, he must do something that culturally he naturally doesn't do.

I know personally of a Pastor from Milan in Italy who went to a bar with some friends among whom was a Romanian woman. In Romania, it is a shocking thing for a Christian to drink any alcohol, let alone a Pastor. This Italian Pastor bought a beer which completely scandalised this Romanian lady (he didn't realise the offence until after). Upon hearing this, the Pastor decided that although for him, it is within his right to have a beer, he laid down that right and bought coffee or tea instead. He gave up his freedom for the concern of another, and this is what it means to love and care more about the welfare of others than one's own. This principle is also repeated in Romans 14, where Paul lays out the same matter to the church in Rome. Firstly, there is to be no contempt for those who refrain from things which, although lawful, aren't expedient for them:

> *The one who eats is not to regard with contempt the one who does not eat, and the one who does not eat is not to judge the one who eats, for God has accepted him… But you, why do you judge your brother? Or you again, why do you regard your brother with contempt? For we will all stand before the judgment seat of God.*

- Romans 14:3, 10

Secondly, one is giving serious consideration to these matters to be fully convinced in one's own mind:

> *One person regards one day above another, another regards every day alike. Each person must be fully convinced in his own mind… The faith which you have, have as your own conviction before God. Happy is he who does not condemn himself in what he approves.*

- Romans 14:5, 22

Thirdly, one is to avoid those things which could cause one's brother to stumble so that you are not creating a stumbling block for your brother.

> Therefore let us not judge one another anymore, but rather determine this—not to put an obstacle or a stumbling block in a brother's way. I know and am convinced in the Lord Jesus that nothing is unclean in itself; but to him who thinks anything to be unclean, to him it is unclean. For if because of food your brother is hurt, you are no longer walking according to love. Do not destroy with your food him for whom Christ died. Therefore do not let what is for you a good thing be spoken of as evil... It is good not to eat meat or to drink wine, or to do anything by which your brother stumbles.
>
> *- Romans 14:13-16, 21*

And lastly, as the saying goes, if in doubt, don't:

> But he who doubts is condemned if he eats, because his eating is not from faith; and whatever is not from faith is sin.
>
> *- Romans 14:23*

In the Kingdom of God, there is only one culture that should prevail – that is the Kingdom culture. Namely, love for one another. Let love be the rallying cry today!

> Do nothing from selfishness or empty conceit, but with humility of mind regard one another as more important than yourselves; do not merely look out for your own personal interests, but also for the interests of others.
>
> *- Philippians 2:3-4*

CHAPTER THREE:
INTERNET – THE
NEW BABEL?

W ith every successive generation brings with it each its own challenges, dilemmas, and problems. This generation these last days is what Daniel 12:4 speaks about where it is written 'many will go back and forth, and knowledge will increase.' Of course, the most significant resource available now regarding knowledge is, in fact, the internet. What a wonderful blessing it is in modern times to be able to in instant communication with someone on the other side of the planet. Or if somehow some information about a particular thing is urgently needed how readily the solution would be available from just a click of a button! However, there is something very sinister about it all.

Be of sober spirit, be on the alert. Your adversary, the devil, prowls around like a roaring lion, seeking someone to devour.

- 1 Peter 5:8

Although the internet is a great resource and an absolute necessity in this technological age, it is one of the most dangerous snares laid by the devil himself. Of course, it is not at all being inferred that no good can come from it, for it is a great resource that can be used by Christians, but there are some areas of concern that must be highlighted with this age of connection.

The Internet Is Crawling With Pornography

The fact remains that according to the Huffington post not only do porn sites get more visitors each month than Netflix, Amazon, and Twitter combined, but 30 per cent of all data transferred across the Internet is porn.[1]

Think about that for just a moment. Nearly one-third of everything viewed on the internet is pornography. That's unbelievable! You must also bear in mind that it is also written that 70% of men and 30% of women watch pornography.[2]

Of course, the Bible teaches that the whole world is under the sway of the wicked one (1 John 5:19) and that the darkness is overwhelming the people. Think about this; also, there is a particular rule on the internet. It goes something like this, 'if it exists, there's a porn version of it.' You would apply this so-called rule on whatever innocent thing you could think of, and there will be a pornographic version. This is a generation of technology but assuredly not before being a generation of perverts. The real shocking thing is that it is not just the world that is contending with this muck but also many Bible-believing Christians. It is written:

> *'Fifty percent of Christian men and 20% of Christian women say they are addicted to pornography. And the most popular day of the week for viewing porn is Sunday.'*[3]

If you meditate on that, it should horrify you. Christians have not only watched pornography, but they do it on the same day as going to Church. They go to Church, lift up holy hands, then go home and flood their eyes and minds with filth straight from the pits.

"Have you not done this to yourself
By your forsaking the Lord your God
When He led you in the way?
"But now what are you doing on the road to Egypt,
To drink the waters of the Nile?
Or what are you doing on the road to Assyria,
To drink the waters of the Euphrates?

- Jeremiah 2:17-18

These people turned to their sin while God was leading them. They were rescued and delivered from this world with all its perversions, but there they are going back to their old sins and their old lifestyles.

For these people have been trapped, pulled in by some succulently alluring bait and have been ensnared by the devil. Bound by lusts and habits they can't break. It is all fuelled relentlessly by the internet, inflaming the passions of the flesh.

Social Networking Is Binding

Consider another part of the World Wide Web, which is almost as addictive as pornography itself, the social network. Many people cannot bear to go one day without them. They check their phones more than several times a day, to check perhaps if someone has emailed, or whether a message from Facebook has come through, or a tweet has been retweeted, etc. The real problem for Christians is that these things cause one to rely on and depend on people over the internet instead of leaning on God!

"Woe to the rebellious children," declares the Lord,
"Who execute a plan, but not Mine,
And make an alliance, but not of My Spirit,
In order to add sin to sin;
Who proceed down to Egypt
Without consulting Me,

To take refuge in the safety of Pharaoh
And to seek shelter in the shadow of Egypt!
"Therefore the safety of Pharaoh will be your shame
And the shelter in the shadow of Egypt, your humiliation.

- Isaiah 30:1-3

The Israelites, who were the people of God, went to Pharaoh and Egypt for help when they were in distress or trouble. Pharaoh represents the devil, and Egypt represents the world. When a person is hooked on social media, do you know what happens? When they are upset, need help or answers, rather than going straight to God in prayer, they go straight to their friends on the internet instead! But God said *'since you trust in Pharaoh, therefore, Pharaoh will be your shame!'* And I have learnt from painful experience that when you lean on anything other than the Lord, then He will always bring that thing down so that your trust in that thing or person will be your very shame!

Dependency on something other than God is an incredible sin. It's basically idolatry of the mind. To feel good about yourself, you need to have this thing (or person) in your life. When you don't have access to it, you start to suffer from withdrawal, which is a sign of its power and hold over you. This is very serious and dangerous.

Thus says the Lord,
"Cursed is the man who trusts in mankind
And makes flesh his strength,
And whose heart turns away from the Lord.
"For he will be like a bush in the desert
And will not see when prosperity comes,
But will live in stony wastes in the wilderness,
A land of salt without inhabitant.
"Blessed is the man who trusts in the Lord
And whose trust is the Lord.
"For he will be like a tree planted by the water,
That extends its roots by a stream
And will not fear when the heat comes;

But its leaves will be green,
And it will not be anxious in a year of drought
Nor cease to yield fruit.

- Jeremiah 17:5-8

God is talking about someone who puts all their faith in people as they stop trusting in God alone. But God would have His people lean only on Him. When believing in people, they live in the desert. There is no life because God withdraws from them. He does this to demonstrate that He will not be second in love and affection. He is a Jealous God (*See Exodus 34:14*)! However, when a person repents and allows Him to remove these idols, they will be planted by living water, God will not at any point tolerate idols among His people. Think about this, God's worst grief in the Old Testament was not the idolatry of the pagan nations but was the idolatry of His people. God's problem was with Israel. Today God's controversy is not with the world but with the Church.

Instant Access Widens The Net

Part of the most significant danger of the internet is the fact that it can be accessed at any time from almost any place. Nowadays, kids have online access straight from their phones. And because phones are password protected, there are no snooping parents to keep an eye on the things that their children are viewing. Children can watch pornography right in your perimeter and yet you wouldn't even know about it. Quite a terrifying thing to think about.

The enemy has made this service available to portable devices so that it is easier and far more likely to enter your home. He used to be more outrageous in Bible times, but these days he is a sneaking devil, enraged he seeks to bring as much confusion and disorder into Christian homes as possible, and this is one of those mediums. The author (although at the time of writing is both single and childless) is persuaded that children should not have free access to the internet via portable devices.

Now before satan appear to be glorified and paraded up, it must be said that the truth of the matter is that God is in full control. Yet these times are so dangerous that God through Paul forewarns of these days:

But realize this, that in the last days difficult times will come. For men will be lovers of self, lovers of money, boastful, arrogant, revilers, disobedient to parents, ungrateful, unholy, unloving, irreconcilable, malicious gossips, without self-control, brutal, haters of good, treacherous, reckless, conceited, lovers of pleasure rather than lovers of God.

- 2 Timothy 3:1-4

The reason He warns the Church so clearly is because He wants His people to take action.

Finally, be strong in the Lord and in the strength of His might. Put on the full armor of God, so that you will be able to stand firm against the schemes of the devil. For our struggle is not against flesh and blood, but against the rulers, against the powers, against the world forces of this darkness, against the spiritual forces of wickedness in the heavenly places.

- Ephesians 6:10-12

God wants His people to be prepared for the battle – but some are ensnared already.

Some People Are Always On Their Phones

There are those Christians who talk about how much the Lord means to them yet whenever they are found, they are found on their phones and not on their knees, such a terrible tragedy! Folks, it ought not to be this way at all! For a Christian to spend much more time on the phone rather than with God is plain idolatry and quite frankly should be unthinkable! Evidently, it is not.

Where your heart is, that is where your true affections lie, and what is in your heart will be demonstrated through your actions. You can, for instance; talk about how much the Lord means everything to you. Yet if you never pray, never read the Bible but rather you are continuously found on your phone then the words of your mouth and the actions you commit both clearly contradict each other. You are not living according to the words of your mouth.

The problem is that if this is you, your phone has your heart. Only the Lord Jesus Christ should have your heart. Only the Lord should be the centre of your affections.

However, before proceeding any further, there is more to be said. I need to share something about my personal life; this is so that you will hear my heart on the matter. Not as a preacher or a holier-than-thou somebody but because I am a simple Christian who loves Jesus and have escaped from the same snares written here. I have failed God the most in this area of my life. Which is the reason why not only am I passionate about this but also have the right to talk about it with you.

While at Bible College, I got addicted to speaking with people on the internet. During this period, my love for God started to wane because now at this moment of my life if I were emotionally in need, I would go to my internet friends. I forgot God! To make things much worse, I became particularly attached to a particular friend to the point of harassment and obsession. I gave this person an impossibly hard time. I became very dark, and I was always on my phone, and I lost interest in anything other than spending time with this person. The relationship led me into grave sin, which I discovered led me into a pit, a bottomless and dark pit. God rescued me by putting enmity between this person and me. Remember how I said that the thing you trust will become the thing that shames you? This was happening to me. Yet despite being freed from this relationship, I still had ties to the internet. I was still talking with people, and from time to time, I would fall into pornography.

God severely disciplined me, both through an emotional breakdown on many online relationships and through relationships at the Bible College. He broke me so much to show me how much He wanted me all to Himself. I came off of Facebook, and God broke my phone with its access to the internet and apps such as WhatsApp. So I had no medium in which to speak with people. I even got rid of my laptop, and this was following Matthew 5:27-30.

So what was the result of that? It was so glorious. I had no distractions, no idols any more holding the barrier between Him and me. I gained my prayer life again, and my zeal for God was increasing as before. Unfortunately, I also had to break through the many Christian voices. They were saying to me that my idea of cutting these things out of my life was extreme. This hurt and disturbed me a little. But I had to shake them off and do what God was telling me to do. My phone remained broken for eight months. Afterwards, God allowed me to have my phone back. Yet not before destroying the idolatry it created.

This is a great sin committed by so many sincere Christians who really don't understand the pain they cause God.

"Can a virgin forget her ornaments,
Or a bride her attire?
Yet My people have forgotten Me
Days without number.

- Jeremiah 2:32

If Christians really understood how much they hurt Him, they would not cling to their idols at all. Instead, they would be terribly ashamed of them. The question therefore remains: what are you going to do about what you have just read? What does this mean for you?

It is so essential that one does not allow the vices of cyberspace to ensnare. Most would say that a person needs to be balanced for this is the way to victory. That one ought to use the good of the internet and avoid the bad. Well said! If indeed, you are able. But should you fall into sin and are trapped like I was then I would advise you, at least for a little while only, to do as I have done.

People will say, '*don't be extreme, be balanced*' which can be useful, there is no denying that. But Jesus **never ever** tells us to be balanced.

> "*If your hand or your foot causes you to stumble, cut it off and throw it from you; it is better for you to enter life crippled or lame, than to have two hands or two feet and be cast into the eternal fire. If your eye causes you to stumble, pluck it out and throw it from you. It is better for you to enter life with one eye, than to have two eyes and be cast into the fiery hell.*
>
> *- Matthew 18:8-9*

If you have anything in your life that leads you into sin – get it out of your life. Being balanced is good but, where you are unable to be so, the best option is not to have it at all. And yes, the internet is vital for today – but so many Christians are in idolatry. They are in bondage. And God has set me free, so He can and also wants to set you free. God loves you so much that He sent Jesus to die for you. He did it so that you could be set free. The Lord wants to give you peace and total freedom!

> *So if the Son makes you free, you will be free indeed.*
>
> *- John 8:36*

Everything here in this world will one day burn up, including the internet. Only God remains forever. Choose life!

> *But the day of the Lord will come like a thief, in which the heavens will pass away with a roar and the elements will be destroyed with intense heat, and the earth and its works will be burned up. Since all these things are to be destroyed in this way, what sort of people ought you to be in holy conduct and godliness, looking for and hastening the coming of the day of God, because of which*

the heavens will be destroyed by burning, and the elements will melt with intense heat! But according to His promise we are looking for new heavens and a new earth, in which righteousness dwells.

- 2 Peter 3:10-13

CHAPTER FOUR: THE ENEMY WITHIN

Today, there has arisen an ancient problem. Of course, God knew before hand that such things would happen and has warned His people about it.

Turn Your footsteps toward the perpetual ruins;
The enemy has damaged everything within the sanctuary.
Your adversaries have roared in the midst of Your meeting place;
They have set up their own standards for signs.

- Psalm 74:3-4

This Psalm has never been more applicable. The enemy knows that the Church of Jesus Christ can never be overcome, so he seeks to infiltrate the Church with his own servants.

For such men are false apostles, deceitful workers, disguising themselves as apostles of Christ. No wonder, for even Satan disguises himself as an angel of light. Therefore it is not surprising if his servants also disguise themselves as servants of righteousness, whose end will be according to their deeds.

- 2 Corinthians 11:13-15

It should not surprise you then if the official Church backslides and apostates. satan is sending his false apostles and ministers into the Church to undermine the Church and destroy her from the inside. Think about Methodism which movement has its roots in revival through the fearless preaching of a godly John Wesley. Yet in July 2018, his original chapel was used by Christians to hold a service of Celebration' affirming LGBT+ lifestyles for Christians, followed by attendance at Pride Bristol and the minister defended the service. Rev Mandy Briggs said: "We are allowed to hold appropriate services where trustees have agreed… but I want to stress that we do not marry gay couples and we are not allowed to bless gay marriages."[1]

The Reverend affirmed that they do not have direct involvement, but by allowing it to happen in their chapel, they are showing their approval of such things. The Bible is evident in its views regarding homosexuality. Just read Romans 1:26-27, 1 Corinthians 6:9 & Jude 7.

So how did Wesley's chapel come to be used for such things? How could the movement he started have so turned from the truth it was founded on? Folks, these things don't happen by accident. There was a breach into which demonically sent men have come through into the Church from the world, bringing with them the values of the world. But it is often forgotten that friendship with the world means that you are an enemy of God (*James 4:4*)!

In the Church of England, according to the BBC news, fourteen clergies in same-sex marriages have called on Bishops to do more to include gay people in the life of the Church. In a letter to the Sunday Times, they said they wanted to eventually see gay couples allowed to marry in Church.[2] They don't just want gay marriage; they want to bring it right into the heart of the Church! Or consider some of the words of Lord Carey a former Archbishop of Canterbury concerning three-parent babies:

"Turning our backs on these advances is uncaring and unloving. We live in an exciting time for medical research

and we must support caring scientists and doctors with the resources and proper regulations to do their work."3

Even though it is playing God, there is a hidden agenda that is very sinister. Such work has an appearance of wanting to bring cures to genetic illnesses, but the author believes that the aim is really to make it possible for homosexuals and lesbians to have children with the DNA of both partners.

There is a growing fad among Churches to turn the house of God, into an entertaining arena. Trying to please carnal members, people who would not be interested in attending Christian services otherwise. An example is this habit of selling alcoholic drinks after the service. Changing the atmosphere, from one of worship to one of a nightclub. It is irreverent and disrespectful to God. Consider the following:

> *The Lord then spoke to Aaron, saying, "**Do not drink wine or strong drink, neither you nor your sons with you, when you come into the tent of meeting, so that you will not die**—it is a perpetual statute throughout your generations—and so as to make a distinction between the holy and the profane, and between the unclean and the clean, and so as to teach the sons of Israel all the statutes which the Lord has spoken to them through Moses."*

> *- Leviticus 10:8-11 (Emphasis added)*

Yet even more shocking is, the 'Taste Ramadan[4]' evening hosted by a church in Yardley which included representatives from a Baptist and an Anglican Church. It is not a bad thing to show hospitality to people of other faiths – a kind gesture following in the footsteps of the Master Jesus Christ who ate and drank with sinners. But to celebrate and host for Ramadan – is an entirely different matter. Ramadan is celebrated by Muslims to remember Muhammad's revelation of the Qur'an. So by taking part in this celebration, they are giving approval to this holy book of theirs.

It is a very heavy and weighty subject no doubt about it. It must be mentioned because the enemy is moving into the church and infiltrating it. But what does this actually mean? Should the Christian give up in defeat and sit on the ground in self-pity? God forbid! The Bible makes it very clear!

*I also say to you that you are Peter, and upon this rock **I will build My church; and the gates of Hades will not overpower it.***

- Matthew 16:18 (Emphasis added)

However, it must be understood that God is talking about the holy remnant. The enemy has come in and is making a mess everywhere, but he cannot touch the spiritual man! He cannot reach the man or the woman who is shut in with Jesus in the secret closet and devouring His Word.[5]

We know that no one who is born of God sins; but He who was born of God keeps him, and the evil one does not touch him.

- 1 John 5:18

If you look at the life of Balaam[6] *(please see Numbers 22-24)*, you will see how he was called upon by Barak to curse the people of God. This was a satanic strategy to bring down the congregation of the Lord from without. Yet however, God utterly refused to allow it because He was a wall of fire protecting Israel! The enemy knows he can't touch the Church from without because he knows Who's guarding the gate. So what does he do instead?

While Israel remained at Shittim, the people began to play the harlot with the daughters of Moab. For they invited the people to the sacrifices of their gods, and the people ate and bowed down to their gods. So Israel joined themselves to Baal of Peor, and the Lord was angry against Israel.

- Numbers 25:1-3

How is it that the people of God were so easily seduced into immorality? The New Testament sheds some interesting light on the subject for us:

But I have a few things against you, because you have there some who hold the teaching of Balaam, who kept teaching Balak to put a stumbling block before the sons of Israel, to eat things sacrificed to idols and to commit acts of immorality.

- Revelation 2:14

Balaam failed to attack the Israelites from the outside, so instead, he uses trickery by infiltrating the tribes to turn their hearts away from that which pleases God. In the same way, the enemy is seeking to destroy churches in the West by intermingling them with the world so that they lose their power as a testimony for God and a light for a lost world. He seeks to undermine the Church from the inside out. However, the enemy will not ultimately triumph. For the church will arise in purity and holiness!

*Let us rejoice and be glad and give the glory to Him, for the marriage of the Lamb has come and **His bride has made herself ready**."*

- Revelation 19:7 (Emphasis added)

What is needed today is for Christians in love and with tears to make a stand for holiness – separation from the world and consecration of their lives unto God alone.

CHAPTER FIVE:
DESPISING THE WORD

The Word of God is to be respected above all other books for no other book comes close to being divinely inspired. No other book has been more loved or hated.

The prophet who has a dream may relate his dream, but let him who has My word speak My word in truth. What does straw have in common with grain?" declares the Lord. "Is not My word like fire?" declares the Lord, "and like a hammer which shatters a rock?

- Jeremiah 23:28-29

God is saying that when anyone speaks His Word, he must do it with the truth. Not only that, but he cannot alter it to please the demands of people. Reminding the reader that although He speaks divine life, is full of love and compassion His Word is very often hard and very strong. Unfortunately, a condition of the society of today has started to have a significant impact in the Church. This is post-modernism or as it can be called: relativism. In the dictionary, relativism is defined as:

'The doctrine that knowledge, truth, and morality exist in relation to culture, society, or historical context, and are not absolute'1

...f course, the Church acknowledges contrary to this regarding ...er doctrine. However, the bottom line of this worldview is that everything is based on a person's feelings. If it feels right for the individual then for them, it is right. This is the problem in the Church. A lot of Christians are so concerned with feelings that when God's Word comes forth with unction and anointing, like a fire or a hammer, they cannot handle it. If it is an encouragement, then they gladly receive the Word, if it's about love or peace. Yet when they are confronted about their sins, or challenged because of an idol, they get angry and refuse to listen.

> For this is a rebellious people, false sons,
> Sons who refuse to listen
> To the instruction of the Lord;
> Who say to the seers, "You must not see visions";
> And to the prophets, "You must not prophesy to us what is right,
> Speak to us pleasant words,
> Prophesy illusions.
> "Get out of the way, turn aside from the path,
> Let us hear no more about the Holy One of Israel."
>
> - Isaiah 30:9-11

You cannot possibly grow in your relationship with God without Him hurting your feelings from time to time. The Lord doesn't speak hard things because He wants to make you feel bad but rather because He loves you, and as a Father, He has to discipline you (*See Hebrews 12:6-8*). Contrary to the popular opinion in the Church, God's love is not about feelings, hugs, etc. His love goes deeper than that. Then again, because many are so selfish that they only want to receive the love that makes them feel nice rather than the love that rescues from sin. I don't really know of a better illustration than to use an experience from my own life. Yet before I set forth this example, I must say something about myself so you can see my heart. I have since my early Christian days understood the justice of God and His holiness; it is only however in reasonably recent times since writing this book that I have started to understand about His love and compassion, even towards me. So with this in mind, I must say that I have before judged people and made some terrible mistakes, even with some good intentions. Now I am more balanced in this I seek to speak God's Word as He wants me to.

I was once asked to lead a prayer meeting – and God told me to speak about holiness. I think this is because sometimes Christians believe that praying loudly and super spiritually will get their voices heard on high. So I spoke briefly from Isaiah 1:10-17 exhorting them to put things right with God and each other. I reminded them that God is indeed a loving Father but He is also a holy God, and I didn't feel to be particularly harsh as in my heart I wanted them to understand how we have to approach God morally speaking.

Later I found out through a good friend (someone who does hear God's voice, so this discouragement was unexpected and upsetting for me) that someone was offended with me for this evening. Apparently what I said was too hard and the person concerned felt judged by me. My friend gave me advice because he loves me and doesn't want me to make such a mistake again (*God told me to speak about this*). He suggested I should not be so strong and that I should be careful about how I present the truth. I was incredibly down about this as I actually didn't want to bring the hard Word, but I knew God wanted me to.

Afterwards, it occurred to me why a person in this situation could have felt judged, even though it was not the case. Often we feel judged during a certain kind of preaching because our own conscience condemns us. The reason for this is because we know we have a sin we need to repent of, and the Holy Spirit uses the Word to bring to light an area in our lives that He doesn't like. The speaking of the authoritative Word of God comes as a hammer to break the heart and arouse the conscience with the Holy Spirit to bring knowledge and conviction of sin, the conscience within us gnaws at us giving us the sensation of feeling judged. When really we aren't judged at all, but instead we start to become bothered by this area, and we in our hard hearts attribute this to the *'judge-mental preacher.'*

Thus says the Lord,

"Heaven is My throne, and the earth is My footstool.
Where then is a house you could build for Me?
And where is a place that I may rest?
"For My hand made all these things,
Thus all these things came into being," declares the Lord.
"But to this one I will look,
To him who is humble and contrite of spirit, and **who**
trembles at My word.

- Isaiah 66:1-2 (Emphasis added)

The problem with many Christians today is that they treat God's Word so lightly. They claim to delight in it but when it comes in power how it is suddenly an altogether different story! When the challenge or confrontation comes, they tend to justify themselves instead of listening to it and correcting their lives.

And He said to them, "You are those who justify yourselves in
the sight of men, but God knows your hearts; for that which is
highly esteemed among men is detestable in the sight of God.

- Luke 16:15

This malady is widespread you can see it by the preaching that goes on in the churches. Here in England, seldom or very rarely will you ever hear a challenging message. Pastors and preachers are often guilty of speaking only what the people want to hear rather than what God actually has to say. This is because the Church has allowed the culture around her to determine how she views and interprets the Word of life. People tend to cherry-pick the Bible, they listen to what they want to, and they then often ignore those problematic parts. You need to take the Word of God in its entirety – not holding some teachings as being superior to others. This is a wicked generation that hates God, hates Christ and hates

His Bible. So with that in mind then why on earth are Christians so ashamed of His Words? Why do they care more about offending people rather than offending God?

> *How can you believe, when you receive glory from one another and you do not seek the glory that is from the one and only God?*
>
> *- John 5:44*

Let us not be afraid of the hard truth or correction. Let us face up to the mouth of God and stop hiding behind political correctness and counselling. Let us stop allowing our culture to shape our perception of the Bible.

> *For whoever is ashamed of Me and My words in this adulterous and sinful generation, the Son of Man will also be ashamed of him when He comes in the glory of His Father with the holy angels."*
>
> *- Mark 8:38*

The culture around you does not define who you are in Christ. If you are a Christian, you are a son or daughter of the Living God. The Kingdom that you are a part of is far more superior than any kingdom or society here!

CHAPTER SIX: APATHY – THE KILLER OF CHRISTIAN PASSION

There are two types of Christians that the devil really hates, those who pray and those who speak. He would instead much rather have them play and sleep! His biggest agent to disable a praying and evangelising Christian is to kill his passion and fire.

John Bunyan adequately wrote about this in the famous Pilgrim's Progress. In one scene, there is a wall with fire, and there is a man who is trying to put out the fire by throwing a lot of water at it – to no avail. This is because, behind the wall, there is another man who is secretly casting oil at the wall to maintain the fire. The fire is God's work in a heart, the one throwing water is the devil and the one throwing oil secretly is Christ:

Then said Christian: What means this?

The Interpreter answered: This is Christ, who continually, with the oil of his grace, maintains the work already begun in the heart: by the means of which, notwithstanding what the devil can do, the souls of His people prove gracious still. And in that you saw that the man stood behind the wall to maintain the fire, that is to teach you that it is hard for the tempted to see how this work of grace is maintained in the soul.[1]

God is always working in the heart of the Christian. No amount of force from hell will ever be able to stop God. Nor should the Christian feel that because God is the one who works in the heart that he or she has no responsibility in the matter whatsoever. God does not use people; instead, He chooses to work with people. For example, you may ask God to help you catch the bus on time, yet, if you remain on your sofa in your house, then you will by no means catch the bus. It will not come to your living room! You have to make an effort to go to the bus station, and God will do the rest and help you.

> For just as the body without the spirit is dead, so also faith without works is dead.
>
> *- James 2:26*

Where might one see this principle in the Word of God? It can be found in Leviticus 6:

> Then the Lord spoke to Moses, saying, "Command Aaron and his sons, saying, 'This is the law for the burnt offering: the burnt offering itself shall remain on the hearth on the altar all night until the morning, and the fire on the altar is to be kept burning on it. The priest is to put on his linen robe, and he shall put on undergarments next to his flesh; and he shall take up the ashes to which the fire reduces the burnt offering on the altar and place them beside the altar. Then he shall take off his garments and put on other garments, and carry the ashes outside the camp to a clean place. **The fire on the altar shall be kept burning on it. It shall not go out, but the priest shall burn wood on it every morning; and he shall lay out the burnt offering on it, and offer up in smoke the fat portions of the peace offerings on it. Fire shall be kept burning continually on the altar; it is not to go out.**
>
> *- Leviticus 6:8-13 (Emphasis added)*

This was to be done in the temple where the altar is. As you can see, it was the job of the Priest to keep the fire going by adding the fuel. These very things are all written as examples for Christians today (*1 Corinthians 10:11*). The fire represents God the Holy Spirit (*See Hebrews 12:29*) and the Temple represents the body of a believer (*See 1 Corinthians 6:19*). The Bible clearly teaches the Priesthood of all believers (*See Revelation 1:6*).

So although God burns within the believer, it is their job to provide the wood! It is never God's intention that the fire 'should ever die on the contrary ***it is not to go out*** (*Leviticus 6:13*)'.

A relationship is where two people make a conscious effort to maintain a friendship. If it is only one person doing all the work, it can hardly be considered a relationship! You will not have God's fire if you make no effort. That beautiful friendship with the Lord must be maintained and cared for. And it is the death of this care that causes the fire to go out in many lives. People who once had Holy Ghost zeal for the things of God are now only a shell of who they once were, and it is so sad. How does this happen to people? How could they turn away from God?

> *Take care, brethren, that there not be in any one of you an evil, unbelieving heart that falls away from the living God. But encourage one another day after day, as long as it is still called "Today," so that none of you will be hardened by the deceitfulness of sin.*
>
> *- Hebrews 3:12-13*

Here the Bible gives us a couple of the reasons, though there are others.

1. An unbelieving heart.

2. Hardening by the deceitfulness of sin.

True faith must be appropriately placed on God, for a man may half-heartedly serve the Lord Christ and yet because his heart is divided it will pull him away as he is not able to maintain his walk. So it is with the man or woman who has a sin that they cling to. A hard heart is the result of someone who refuses to repent to the point where they give themselves over to the sin. Where they had a "love" for God, through other loves, what should have been one great love for the Lord is displaced.

There is another problem that comes to attack every person that set their hearts on walking fully with Jesus: the spirit of spiritual slumber. A demonic strategy to undermine the fighting Christian's focus and causes them to give up the fight.

"You're tired!"

"Don't pray today, you are too busy now!"

"Relax your standards, God is not that hard!"

All you beasts of the field,
All you beasts in the forest,
Come to eat.
His watchmen are blind,
All of them know nothing.
All of them are mute dogs unable to bark,
Dreamers lying down, who love to slumber;
And the dogs are greedy, they are not satisfied.
And they are shepherds who have no understanding;
They have all turned to their own way,
Each one to his unjust gain, to the last one.
"Come," they say, "let us get wine, and let us drink heavily of
strong drink;
And tomorrow will be like today, only more so."

- Isaiah 56:9-12

The beasts here are like demon powers. The watchmen represent the Christian that has fallen asleep and is playing around and flirting with his sin. He is in a terrible condition, but his only focus is on his pleasures, not on what the beasts are doing. There are so many Christians that are asleep. satan is terrorizing the world, and instead of standing guard watching out for him, believers are flirting with the world and their sins. Consider the following:

Therefore, I exhort the elders among you, as your fellow elder and witness of the sufferings of Christ, and a partaker also of the glory that is to be revealed, shepherd the flock of God among you, exercising oversight not under compulsion, but voluntarily, according to the will of God; and not for sordid gain, but with eagerness; nor yet as lording it over those allotted to your charge, but proving to be examples to the flock. And when the Chief Shepherd appears, you will receive the unfading crown of glory. You younger men, likewise, be subject to your elders; and all of you, clothe yourselves with humility toward one another, for God is opposed to the proud, but gives grace to the humble.

Therefore humble yourselves under the mighty hand of God, that He may exalt you at the proper time, casting all your anxiety on Him, because He cares for you. Be of sober spirit, be on the alert. Your adversary, the devil, prowls around like a roaring lion, seeking someone to devour.

- 1 Peter 5:1-8

As you can see, there is a proper way for the Christian to live concerning the Church. But in Isaiah 56 the shepherds (or Pastors it should be said) are not doing much better. God has a lot of displeasure against all of this.

Be delayed and wait,
Blind yourselves and be blind;
They become drunk, but not with wine,
They stagger, but not with strong drink.
For the Lord has poured over you a spirit of deep sleep,
He has shut your eyes, the prophets;

And He has covered your heads, the seers.

- Isaiah 29:9-10

God holds His people responsible not only for their condition but also for the state of the society around them. The buck stops with the Church. At this moment, the Church needs to wake up from her sleep of apathy. God wants to transform this world, and the author believes that God primarily intends to do it through His body the Church.

In my personal life, when I first became a Christian, I had such a hunger for Jesus that nothing could take it away. My prayer life was at its peak with two to three hours a day. I also read the Bible and went to bed each night listening to a sermon. During this time I got the call to go to Bible College – in the first year, I got up every day at 6 am to pray before the day started (this was because the allocated hour for a quiet time was not long enough). Yet during this time, I began to get physically tired.

Because I had a lot of zeal without knowledge, I used an occasion to rebuke Christians for their apathy towards prayer (I had the right heart, but I did the wrong thing) which resulted in completely destroying my fire and passion through the negative responses I received. This situation broke me as I was incredibly wounded and fragile. Because I felt the shame of my zealous actions, I stopped believing that God had a fire for me, so consequently, I let it die.

It was during this delicate time that the enemy took full advantage of my vulnerable position. He laid a snare for my life that nearly ended my Christian walk forever. I was entrapped in sin, and all my fire was gone. I tried very hard to get my passion back because I could feel that I was dead inside, when the death came over me I had this powerful sense that life had gone. I had been ensnared in sin and idolatry, and because of it, I was never able to find God. I prayed so much that I began despairing of living because the Lord was completely withholding His presence from me. He never left me, but it felt like He did during this period. In fact, on quite a few occasions, I would scream at God at the top of my voice for forgetting me and abandoning me (*He did not*). I had contemplated suicide a few times. Dying was much better for me than living without God. The late Pastor David Wilkerson said the following:

> "*There is nothing worse than I can think of for a man of God or for a woman of God than to lose the anointing of God, and be dead and have the knowledge that something is wrong.*"[2]

I can say that that statement is entirely 100% true. The devil even once told me during this dark period:

"*You will never ever get your relationship with God back.*"

The depression that overshadowed me produced in me such apathy that I could not be bothered to do anything. I could not pray, I could not get any pleasure from reading my Bible, I could not write, I could not study, I could not socialise, etc. I could not do anything. It was God that had to set me free from the pit of despair! God saved me from the paw of satan!

> *Blessed be the Lord,*
> *Who has not given us to be torn by their teeth.*
> *Our soul has escaped as a bird out of the snare of the trapper;*
> *The snare is broken and we have escaped.*
> *Our help is in the name of the Lord,*
> *Who made heaven and earth.*

> *- Psalm 124:6-8*

God brought me to a place of destruction so that the idols I had no longer had any power over me. By destroying them, God was able to raise me from my spiritual sleep and set me back at His side! He delivered me from being torn by the teeth of the devil!

God is willing to do that for all those who are willing to repent and turn their lives over to Him anew. God can set the fire going again in hearts. For He is not looking for a half-hearted, lukewarm people but those who will give Him all their hearts and first love, where God is the chief joy of life because nothing compares to knowing Him and walking with Him in intimacy. A Christian that walks with His Lord is an incredible danger – to the powers of darkness. Rarely will they ever know from what direction calamity will come upon them through such a man or woman of God who prays. Such a Christian is also always active in evangelism, the kingdom of satan, therefore, will decrease, and the glorious Kingdom of Christ will increase. And such it should be.

Today if you are under this kind of spirit, repent of allowing it to dominate your life. You have one life, so do not waste it. If you have in your life, something that is displeasing to God, then give it up. Turn to God even if you don't feel like it. Your feelings will catch up sooner or later, but the Lord will bless you. As you put Him first, the glory of His presence will come to you again.

For the Lord will not abandon His people,
Nor will He forsake His inheritance.
For judgment will again be righteous,
And all the upright in heart will follow it.

- Psalm 94:14-15

CHAPTER SEVEN: THE DECEPTIVE POWER OF FEELINGS

This is a day of feelings. This generation is so emotionally charged that society has created many politically correct rules in order not to offend anyone. Unfortunately, this political correctness has managed to creep its way into the church. This malady is so evil that often, Christians are more concerned with feelings than with the truth.

The enemy knows this all too well and takes full advantage of this fact. Often demobilizing a fighting Christian by getting him or her to focus inwardly rather than outwardly, that is to Christ.

> *Therefore, since we have so great a cloud of witnesses surrounding us, let us also lay aside every encumbrance and the sin which so easily entangles us, and let us run with endurance the race that is set before us, fixing our eyes on Jesus, the author and perfecter of faith, who for the joy set before Him endured the cross, despising the shame, and has sat down at the right hand of the throne of God.*
>
> *- Hebrews 12:1-2*

God is described in many parts of the Bible as a Rock – a rock is not like the dirt or earth around it, which is easily broken and moved. Rock is quite something else altogether. Instead, a rock is durable and completely unchanging. When you try to dig into it, you will not make even so much as one dent.

"For I, the Lord, do not change; therefore you, O sons of Jacob, are not consumed.

- Malachi 3:6

Jesus Christ is the same yesterday, today, and forever.

- Hebrews 13:8

Counsellors and pastoral care do have their place. Nor are emotions overtly evil – the Lord Jesus expressed many feelings. As well as being God, He is the fullest expression of manhood as it should be and the only example of a perfect man. But too much emphasis and value are placed on how one feels.

Many Christians go about with depression because of past failures. They don't feel worthy of God's forgiveness and grace, so they walk through life with feelings of condemnation.

Therefore there is now no condemnation for those who are in Christ Jesus.

- Romans 8:1

This is true, regardless of feelings. Feelings go up and down with every passing day, but the Christian's position in Christ doesn't depend on this. Thanks to God for this beautiful truth. If God's promises were dependent on feelings, then a person would be saved and damned a hundred times over and more. But His faithfulness and kindness towards His people are independent of feelings. That is why the Bible likens God to a Rock, steadfast and sure with no variation or shadow of turning (*James 1:17*).

The enemy who knows the weaknesses of the Christian seeks to exploit them, but the believer must resist him when he comes with his accusing voice.

Submit therefore to God. Resist the devil and he will flee from you.

- James 4:7

The word devil here in Greek is *diabŏlŏs*[1], which means slanderer or false accuser. The enemy, therefore, will slander the believer and accuse them of sin to bring upon them guilt and condemnation. He targets the feelings of the individual, but the believer should not listen to him because he is rightly called the father of lies (*John 8:44*). He seeks to use his own emotions of the believer against him.

> *Therefore if anyone is in Christ, he is a new creature; the old things passed away; behold, new things have come.*

- 2 Corinthians 5:17

On the flipside, there is another danger that is perhaps worse. This is the opposite. On one side, emotions are harmful and can cloud the vision of where one stands with Christ – that is in heavenly places (*Ephesians* 2:6).

The other danger is a false sense of security insomuch as to believe in having a position in Christ when the reality is different. Thinking to be Christ's because of high emotions. Both are dangerous and are both extremes that need to be avoided at all costs.

During worship, there is a growing temptation to put on an act or a show for God. By becoming loud, intense and emotional a person can deceive themselves into thinking that they have a spiritual experience. The Holy Spirit does indeed descend during worship, yet there seems to be a considerable lack of discernment among God's people. The emotions run high during the worship, so it can be thought that it is God the Spirit moving when in reality most of the time it is nothing but emotional heat, a particular problem in Pentecostal circles.

Any bad feelings that come are automatically attributed to the devil. *"If I feel bad about something, then it must be the devil!"* This is incredibly deadly if done without a degree of discernment. The reason for this is that when God chooses to bring to attention something in the life of an individual that is displeasing to Him,

He may well spare feelings but for the most part, God does not get concerned over how the person feels but will discipline them.

> *and you have forgotten the exhortation which is addressed to you as sons, "My son, do not regard lightly the discipline of the Lord, nor faint when you are reproved by Him; for those whom the Lord loves He disciplines, and He scourges every son whom He receives." It is for discipline that you endure; God deals with you as with sons; for what son is there whom his father does not discipline? But if you are without discipline, of which all have become partakers, then you are illegitimate children and not sons.*

> *- Hebrews 12:5-8*

God isn't concerned about feelings as much as He is with holiness.

> *Pursue peace with all people, **and holiness, without which no one will see the Lord.***

> *- Hebrews 12:14 (NKJV) (Emphasis added)*

The other danger is bringing people to Jesus using emotions or an emotional experience. An example of this is the tradition of making an appeal and having the musicians play softly in the background. This is to create an atmosphere and stir people to action through manipulation of the senses, but it is not spiritual. No one can come to God who does not repent of his sin, neither can one come to God except it be a supernatural work of God the Holy Spirit in the heart.

> *No one can come to Me unless the Father who sent Me draws him; and I will raise him up on the last day.*

> *- John 6:44*

Christ's own words indicate that salvation is an act of God. So however emotional one may feel if one has not been raised from the dead to newness of life with the Spirit of God breathing His life in then nothing has happened.

The danger is thinking to be saved because of the high emotions during the meeting. But the most significant proof of a changed life is a changed lifestyle – not the happiness that is felt in the heat of the moment. Like every moment, it passes. But the moment someone receives salvation they receive from God a new heart as they begin to love what they once hated and to hate what they once loved.

> *Then I will sprinkle clean water on you, and you will be clean; I will cleanse you from all your filthiness and from all your idols. Moreover, I will give you a new heart and put a new spirit within you; and I will remove the heart of stone from your flesh and give you a heart of flesh.*
>
> *- Ezekiel 36:25-26*

God cleans them by putting in them a heart that desires after Him. That is how they will be cleansed from their idols. This promise is not at all dependent on feelings. The believer walks by faith, not by feelings.

> *for we walk by faith, not by sight.*
>
> *- 2 Corinthians 5:7*

By bringing people to Christ through emotions is to bring people to a religious experience but through no repentance of sin or turning to Christ truly, the person is in effect being made a two-fold child of hell. These beloved souls are being sent to hell in the name of love. The Church must wake up, the eternal destinies of people hang in the balance.

CHAPTER EIGHT: HOLINESS – THE EVANGELICAL ELEPHANT IN THE ROOM

Holiness is one of those subjects that nobody likes talking about. There is a legalistic approach to holiness, but in general, the masses of Christians and the church at large have about as much interest in the word holiness as the world has in the word repentance. The person comes to God to be forgiven of all sin, but it is often forgotten that there is a way that God expects the person to live.

A highway will be there, a roadway,
And it will be called the Highway of Holiness.
The unclean will not travel on it,
But it will be for him who walks that way,
And fools will not wander on it.

- Isaiah 35:8

All you need to access this path is to have a simple and child-like faith, with open ears and open hearts. It is a highway that is most necessary for every Christian.

> *Pursue peace with all people, and holiness, without which no one will see the Lord.*

> *- Hebrews 12:14 (NKJV)*

If you have no desire in you to live a holy life, you won't make it to heaven. Holiness in Greek here is *hagiasmos*, from the word *hagizō*[1] which means: *consecrate; (mentally) to venerate: - hallow, be holy, sanctify.* So, a Christian must be consecrated; otherwise, he will not see God. See in Greek here is *ŏptŏmai*[2] which means: *to gaze with eyes wide open at something remarkable.*

Therefore, if you don't seek to consecrate your life, you will not be able to gaze at the great and remarkable God with your eyes wide open (*See Exodus 33:20 & Revelation 22:4*).

For you to understand this, I will try to illustrate it for you. I am English and thus being an Englishman I have as my head of state – the Queen. Suppose now that I was invited to spend some time in the presence of her majesty. I would be required to go through a protocol – or a procedure, to be able to meet with her. How I would dress, the appropriate manners I would need when speaking, how to greet her, etc. I would be trained in all of this. I could by no means just get out of bed and in my pyjamas go straight to Buckingham Palace as I am and expect to be admitted. I would need to prepare myself for my meeting with her. If I don't go properly, not only will she reject me but she will refuse to even see me. Jesus spoke about this in a parable:

> Go therefore to the main highways, and as many as you find there, invite to the wedding feast.' Those slaves went out into the streets and gathered together all they found, both evil and good; and the wedding hall was filled with dinner guests.

> "But when the king came in to look over the dinner guests, he saw a man there who was not dressed in wedding clothes, and he said to him, 'Friend, how did you come in here without wedding clothes?' And the man was speechless. Then the king said to the

servants, 'Bind him hand and foot, and throw him into the outer
darkness; in that place there will be weeping and gnashing of
teeth.'

- Matthew 22:9-13

Culturally, one might not understand why the man without
wedding clothes offended the King. For since bringing people into
the wedding hall was a matter of urgency (*See Matthew 22:1-14
for the whole parable*), the King would have provided people with
the right clothing. Similarly, if people come to God through Jesus,
they are covered by His righteousness and holiness. Any who seek
to enter God's presence dressed in their own righteousness (*which
is filthy rags!*) will be finally turned away. God offers them righteous standing with Him as a free gift, any who enter without it
shows that they despise the gift. Unholy people will not see God
because God will refuse to see them.

The Christian does have the boldness to enter the holy place
because of the blood of Jesus, being a son or daughter of God. They
have received the righteousness of Jesus Christ through faith.

Now, before getting into what holiness is, it must be made
known to you what holiness is not. Holiness is not keeping to a
strict set of rules and regulations to please God. This is legalism.
Keeping every letter of the law while inwardly despising the law
is not true holiness. For that only concerns external appearances
and has nothing to do with the heart.

Neither is holiness how much you attend services or go to
Christian meetings. For you can go to hell even if you spend your
life in the church.

Holiness can be simply defined as this statement:

**You can't take the Christian out of the world, but you can
take the world out of the Christian.**

Holiness is simply consecration to God and separation from the world. That's it. A lot of Christians don't have a problem being consecrated to God. It's being separated from the world that they find difficult! Many Christians want to be accepted by the world because holiness is out of fashion with a sin-loving Christ-rejecting world, so, therefore, Christians avoid it. But Jesus warns against having two masters:

"No one can serve two masters; for either he will hate the one and love the other, or he will be devoted to one and despise the other. You cannot serve God and wealth.

- Matthew 6:24

Yet, this is precisely what some Christians try to do. They want heaven but aren't willing to depart from this world, they want the resurrection but aren't ready to bear the cross, and yet this cannot be so. If you are to be a disciple of Jesus, then you must follow Him. And if you are to follow Him, you must surrender your life as He surrendered His life.

the one who says he abides in Him ought himself to walk in the same manner as He walked.

- 1 John 2:6

It is true that many believers fail in this, yet God is merciful to His people and provides all the grace and strength they need to walk in His ways. All He asks for is a willing and obedient heart. The Holy Spirit will continue His work of sanctification. Holiness, however, is not static in a believer. The level of holiness doesn't remain the same. Your love and devotion to Jesus should always be growing just as your distaste from the things of this world also should increase. Holiness is an attitude of the heart – not the external actions. Actions are a result of inner holiness – they are not what makes a person holy of themselves. Tattoos can be used as another example here. When debates with other Christians have happened, I have heard this statement:

"If you want to reach a non-Christian for Jesus that has tattoos, you should really have tattoos."

In that statement alone from the mouths of Christians, one can see the malady of the church today. The concerning thing is that they think they can win the world by being like it. The problem is one of an attitude.

The statement is most certainly not true. If you are the same as them, then why should they have your Jesus in their lives? What difference will He bring if they will become just like you (i.e. the same)? It is the fact that you are different that will attract people to Jesus. You will stand out – you won't blend in and disappear in the background. Darkness cannot drive out darkness. Only light can do that.

Can it be that the people who project this view are themselves afraid of suffering rejection for being different? Every Christian wrestles with this area. Nobody wants to be known as a freak or as a religious nut. But, for those who are willing, God gives the strength to be different. He will bless the one who truly delights to stand alone for Jesus.

It is also not good to convince people by the love that they belong to Christ when they are not pursuing to live a life that is pleasing to God. A man who is born from above will seek to please He Who is from above, that is God. A true Christian is trying to live a life pleasing to God. Once he puts his faith in Jesus Christ, he becomes a new creation. He is made right with God legally, and the Holy Spirit is given to help him grow into holiness. If your character is unholy, you must ask yourself whether you will see the Lord or not. You will not see Him if you don't belong to Him.

CHAPTER NINE: THE MANY FALSE FACES OF JESUS -PART ONE-

No controversial figure in history is more well-known than Jesus Christ. So many people are saying so many different things about Him. Consider the following from late great Gospel singer Keith Green:

'In the eastern religions and all the cults, the world religions they always gave some credit to Jesus Christ. The Muslims say he was a prophet. The Krishnas say he was an incarnation of the Godhead in his age. All these different eastern teachers said he had Christ consciousness. They always use words like Christ consciousness, Christ this, Jesus that. The Buddhists would even say he was a Buddha. He was another incarnation of God like Buddha was. In all my searching I saw all these people were pointing to Jesus.' [1]

Jesus Christ has many faces. Most of them are false for there is only one and can only be one real Jesus. There are many imposters with many things being spoken about Him.

For if one comes and preaches another Jesus whom we have not preached, or you receive a different spirit which you have not received, or a different gospel which you have not accepted, you bear this beautifully.

- 2 Corinthians 11:4

Yet it is only the truth that really matters. What are people saying about Jesus?

Jesus According To Jehovah Witnesses

It is taught by the Watch Tower Society that the identity and person of Jesus Christ differ significantly from what is commonly taught in Churches. There is no belief in the Trinity but that the only Creator God is the Father who is called Jehovah. In their Bible in Genesis 1:1-2, it is written:

'In the beginning God created the heavens and the earth. Now the earth was formless and desolate, and there was darkness upon the surface of the watery deep, and God's active force was moving about the surface of the waters.'[2]

It is clearly taught that the belief of the Holy Spirit or Spirit of God is not a Deity or a living being but rather is a power-force of God and nothing else. As for the Son, it is written in their Bible in John 1:1 the following:

'In the beginning was the Word, and the Word was with God, and the word was a god.'[3]

If Jehovah is the one true God, and there is no Trinity, then why does it say that Jesus was a god? The answer they give can be found in the Watchtower book 'What Does the Bible Really Teach?' The belief is that Jesus was created by Jehovah at the beginning and with Jesus, He created the world. It is written in this book:

'Jesus is Jehovah's most precious Son—and for good reason. He is called "the firstborn of all creation," for he was God's first creation...Jehovah is called a father because he is the Creator, (Isaiah 64:8). Since Jesus was created by God he is called God's Son.'[4]

They believe that Jesus Christ and the Archangel Michael are one and the same. Even the belief that it is *'logical to conclude that*

Michael is none other than Jesus Christ in his heavenly role.'[5] Even the order of pre-eminence between Father and Son is discussed. For it is again written in their publication:

> 'The Bible teaches that the Father is greater than the Son. (Read John 14:28; 1 Corinthians 11:3) Jehovah alone is "God Almighty." (Genesis 17:1) Therefore, he has no equal.'[6]

So the belief is that Jesus is not equal to Jehovah, and he was created by Jehovah before the world began and used him to create the world. His identity is Michael the Archangel.

Jesus According To The Mormon

The Godhead, according to the Mormon, is not Trinitarian, which is the belief in One God Who eternally exists as three Persons. Instead, the view is in three distinct beings. Elohim (the father) is taught to have once been a man in another world. Who through the keeping of the faithful tenants of Mormonism in his world was elevated to the God of this world.[7] Thus the teaching of Mormonism is the possibility of the follower of the Latter-day Saints (LDS), i.e. Mormon, church to become a god of his own world. Consider the following statement from former LDS Mission President Dr Harold Goodman, BYU Professor Mormon:

> 'So you can see why the temple is important to the latter-day saint. Because if he is worthy to go onto the temple and there receive the sacred ordinances and covenants and keep them he can eventually grow into becoming a god himself.'[8]

Both Jesus and Lucifer are taught to be spirit children of Elohim and thus brothers, along with everyone who has been born. For everyone is thought to have existed prior in heaven as spirit children of Elohim:

> 'Thus it is shown that prior to the placing of man upon the earth, how long before we do not know, Christ and Satan, together with the hosts of the spirit-children of God existed as intelligent individuals, possessing power

and opportunity to choose the course they would pursue and the leaders whom they would follow and obey. In that great concourse of spirit-intelligences, the father's plan whereby His children would be advances to the second estate, was submitted and doubtless discussed.'[9]

This abstract was taken from the official LDS website. Jesus, therefore, has a beginning in heaven according to the LDS church. This Jesus was chosen to be the saviour in the divine council with all of Elohim's spirit children. He is therefore according to the LDS church an exalted mortal.

The Jesus (Or Issa) Of Islam

In the Old Testament book of Christianity and Judaism, there is a promise given to Moses by God that He will raise up a prophet like him.

I will raise up a prophet from among their countrymen like you, and I will put My words in his mouth, and he shall speak to them all that I command him. It shall come about that whoever will not listen to My words which he shall speak in My name, I Myself will require it of him.

- Deuteronomy 18:18-19

According to Muslim scholars, the passage refers not to Jesus Christ but rather Muhammad instead.[10] Everything in the Torah points to Muhammad, according to Islam. In the Qur'an, it teaches very clearly that Jesus is clearly a man. According to it He was neither the Son of God nor a god but was merely a prophet. Accordingly, Allah will ask Jesus about this on the day of judgement concerning those who worshipped him:

Surah 5:116 al-Ma'idah
And [beware the Day] when God will
Say: "O Jesus, Son of Mary, did you say
to the people, 'Take me and my mother
as deities besides God?" He will say,

"Exalted are You! It was not for me to
say that to which I have no right. If I had
said it, You would have known it. You
know what is within myself, and I do
not
know what is within Yourself. Indeed, it
is You who is the knower of the unseen.

There the God of Islam questions Jesus on judgement day about those worshipping him, Jesus will reply that he never asked to be worshipped. In fact, Jesus's mission, according to the Qur'an, was to be a forerunner of Muhammad:

Surah 61:6 as-Saff (Edit inserted for clarity mine)
And [mention] when Jesus, the son of
Mary, said, "O children of Israel, indeed
I am the messenger of God to you confirming
what came before me of the Torah
and bringing good tidings of a messenger
to come after me, whose name is
Ahmad (**this is Muhammad**)." But when he came to
them
with clear evidences, they said, "This is
obvious magic."

Jesus, as the Son of God, is a no go area for Muslims because it is seen as another form of polytheism, and they don't hold it to be true. In the Donate Quran from www.donatequran.com, there is an explanation in Surah 43: az-Zukhruf-Ornaments:

'Jesus son of Mary had never said that he was son of God and that the people should worship him. His own was the same teaching which every other Prophet had given: "My Lord as well as your Lord is God: so worship Him alone."

The Holy Spirit, according to the Qur'an, is not the Spirit of God as is understood in Christianity but is actually the angel Gabriel:

Surah 5:110 al-Ma'idah (Emphasis mine)

[The Day] when God will say, "O Jesus,
Son of Mary, remember My favor upon
you and upon your mother **when I supported
you with the Pure Spirit [i.e., the
angel Gabriel]** and you spoke to the people
in the cradle and in maturity; and [remember]
when I taught you writing and
wisdom and the Torah and the Gospel;
and when you designed from clay [what
was] like the form of a bird with My permission,
then you breathed into it, and it
became a bird with My permission; and
you healed the blind [from birth] and the
leper with My permission; and when you
brought forth the dead with My permission;
and when I restrained the Children
of Israel from [killing] you when you
came to them with clear proofs and
those who disbelieved among them said,
"This is not but obvious magic."

Jesus According To The Roman Catholic Church

Roman Catholicism acknowledges the Bible as the Word of God that contains the only truth and revelation from God, but church tradition is said to be on equal grounds as Scripture in terms of authority for life and faith.[11] Jesus Christ is both God the Son, a member of the Trinitarian Godhead and a Man. He became a Man at the conception of the Virgin Mary whereby she received the title 'Mother of God.'[12]

The belief is that although the blood of Jesus cleanses the penitent sinner when he dies a Christian, he is not fit for heaven but must undergo a purification process in purgatory. In their Catechism 1030 it is written:

'All who die in God's grace and friendship, but still imperfectly purified, are indeed assured of their eternal salvation; but after death they undergo purification, so as to achieve the holiness necessary to enter the joy of heaven.' [13]

It is also written in the Catechism 1031 the following:

'The Church gives the name Purgatory to this final purification of the elect, which is entirely different from the punishment of the damned...... As for certain lesser faults, we must believe that, before the final Judgment, there is a purifying fire. He who is truth says that whoever utters blasphemy against the Holy Spirit will be pardoned neither in this age nor in the age to come. From this sentence we understand that certain offenses can be forgiven in this age, but certain others in the age to come.' [14]

Regarding Mary, it is believed that since she gave birth to Jesus she was preserved from all stain of original sin and by a special grace of God committed no sin of any kind during her whole earthly life. [15] (See Catechism 411) So in effect, Mary was sinless. She also ascended into heaven where the Lord made her Queen of all:

...when the course of her earthly life was finished, was taken up body and soul into heavenly glory, and exalted by the Lord as Queen over all things... (Catechism 966) [17]

Now you have read about these different religions it should be known that this chapter is not meant to be exhaustive as there are a great many other books out there that are more comprehensive than this book that is available for purchase. [16] For much more could be written than what is presented to you but you have a little taste here.

CHAPTER TEN: THE MANY FALSE FACES OF JESUS -PART TWO-

S o in light of all of the information in part one about these differing faiths, what is right? The response to each of these four religions is now due. If you are a follower of any of the religions mentioned in the previous chapter, then please read all that is written before you reject it. Truth is important enough to be carefully scrutinised.

Answering The Jw Jesus

The Jehovah Witnesses on their rebuttal of the Trinity say that the actual word Trinity cannot be found in the Bible. Now while that is true, it is not found in the Bible, none of the words used today in English is. You will not find the words Jesus Christ at all in the Bible – as it was written in Hebrew, Aramaic and Greek long before English was developed as a language. However, the concept of the Trinity can indeed be found. For, the Holy Spirit, according to the Bible, is neither a thing nor a force, but He is a Person. He has characteristics that cannot belong to just a mere power force of God Almighty but an actual living Person.

In the same way the Spirit also helps our weakness; for we do not know how to pray as we should, but the Spirit Himself intercedes for us with groanings too deep for words; and He who searches the hearts knows what the mind of the Spirit is, because He intercedes for the saints according to the will of God.

- Romans 8:26-27

The fact that the Holy Spirit has a mind and intercedes (prays) this shows that He speaks and thinks. A personal force wouldn't do either of those but do what God would make it do.

Do not grieve the Holy Spirit of God, by whom you were sealed for the day of redemption.

- Ephesians 4:30

He can be grieved or upset. The capacity to feel emotion belongs only to living beings. A force like electricity cannot feel emotions; it just flows where it is directed! This is clear that He is a Person.

But the Spirit explicitly says that in later times some will fall away from the faith, paying attention to deceitful spirits and doctrines of demons.

- 1 Timothy 4:1

Again, He has the power of speech, so therefore He can express Himself, something a force of God cannot do as it would only do what God would tell it to do. The Spirit then is clearly a Person and not a thing.

In Genesis 1, where it is written: 'Spirit of God,' the Hebrew is אֱלֹהִים רוּחַ[1] which when transliterated is Ruach Elohim. This is literally 'Spirit of God.' There is absolutely no reason whatsoever that the translation of those Hebrew words should be translated as 'God's active force.'

For those whom He foreknew, He also predestined to become conformed to the image of His Son, so that He would be the first-born among many brethren.

- Romans 8:29

Here Jesus Christ is the firstborn. This does not mean that Jesus Christ is the first Son among many, but this is the way God has chosen to bring about His divine order. Consider the following:

Then His mother and His brothers arrived, and standing outside they sent word to Him and called Him. A crowd was sitting around Him, and they said to Him, "Behold, Your mother and Your brothers are outside looking for You." Answering them, He said, "Who are My mother and My brothers?" Looking about at those who were sitting around Him, He said, "Behold My mother and My brothers! For whoever does the will of God, he is My brother and sister and mother."

- Mark 3:31-35

So here it is understandable that Jesus calls those who do God's will His brother and sister and mother. This then is a privilege to those who join themselves to God and is not to be taken in a literal sense that Jesus is the firstborn created Son. It is a privilege bestowed which is entirely to do with status.

For you have not received a spirit of slavery leading to fear again, but you have received a spirit of adoption as sons by which we cry out, "Abba! Father!" The Spirit Himself testifies with our spirit that we are children of God, and if children, heirs also, heirs of God and fellow heirs with Christ, if indeed we suffer with Him so that we may also be glorified with Him.

- Romans 8:15-17

But as many as received Him, to them He gave the right to become children of God, even to those who believe in His name, who were born, not of blood nor of the will of the flesh nor of the will of man, but of God.

- John 1:12-13

Regarding Jesus' Deity and the belief that He was created,

these two passages should be able to speak volumes:

> *For a child will be born to us, a son will be given to us;*
> *And the government will rest on His shoulders;*
> *And His name will be called Wonderful Counselor, Mighty God,*
> *Eternal Father, Prince of Peace.*
> *There will be no end to the increase of His government or of*
> *peace,*
> *On the throne of David and over his kingdom,*
> *To establish it and to uphold it with justice and righteousness*
> *From then on and forevermore.*
> *The zeal of the Lord of hosts will accomplish this.*
>
> *- Isaiah 9:6-7*

Here is an apparent reference to Jesus Christ. Notice the words: 'Eternal Father' and 'Mighty God'. He is here in this passage referred to as the Mighty God Himself.

> *"But as for you, Bethlehem Ephrathah,*
> *Too little to be among the clans of Judah,*
> *From you One will go forth for Me to be ruler in Israel.*
> ***His goings forth are from long ago,***
> ***From the days of eternity."***
>
> *- Micah 5:2 (Emphasis added)*

It is clearly written about the coming of Jesus as He was born in Bethlehem (*See Matthew 2:1, Luke 2:4 & John 7:42*). It says He is from [i.e. the past] the days of eternity. Therefore He existed eternally before and was uncreated. Thus Jesus Christ is Himself Jehovah with the Father and the Holy Spirit. As for Jesus being the same person as Michael, we can see the Michael was an archangel:

> *But Michael the archangel, when he disputed with the devil and*
> *argued about the body of Moses, did not dare pronounce against*
> *him a railing judgment, but said, "The Lord rebuke you!"*
>
> *- Jude 9*

Michael would not rebuke the devil himself but committed it to the Lord. Whereas Jesus Himself did rebuke the devil never saying, 'The Lord rebuke you,' (*See Matthew 4:8-11*) which is entirely different from Michael's response. About Jesus, it is written:

having become as much better than the angels, as He has inherited a more excellent name than they. For to which of the angels did He ever say,

"You are My Son,
Today I have begotten You"?

And again,

"I will be a Father to Him
And He shall be a Son to Me"?

And when He again brings the firstborn into the world, He says,
"And let all the angels of God worship Him."

- Hebrews 1:4-6

So, therefore, you can see God treats Jesus far more different to the angels. Hebrews makes the comparison even greater:

And of the angels He says,
"Who makes His angels winds,
And His ministers a flame of fire."

But of the Son He says,

"Your throne, O God, is forever and ever,
And the righteous scepter is the scepter of His kingdom.
"You have loved righteousness and hated lawlessness;
Therefore God, Your God, has anointed You
With the oil of gladness above Your companions."

- Hebrews 1:7-9

Jesus had a completely different role from any of the angels. In fact, He is to receive worship something the angels hate (*See Rev-*

elation 19:10 & Revelation 22:9). He is superior to them:

> *But to which of the angels has He ever said,*
>
> *"Sit at My right hand,*
> *Until I make Your enemies*
> *A footstool for Your feet"?*
>
> - Hebrews 1:13

Since God requires even the angels to worship Him He, therefore, cannot be the same person as Michael the archangel.

Answering The Mormon Jesus

The idea that a person can become a god is not unique to Mormonism. It was this kind of thinking that led our first parents Adam and Eve to sin in the beginning. The serpent seduced Eve by planting in her a desire with Adam to be as gods.

> *And the serpent said unto the woman, Ye shall not surely die:*
>
> *For God doth know that in the day ye eat thereof, then your eyes shall be opened,* **and ye shall be as gods**, *knowing good and evil.*
>
> - Genesis 3:4-5 (Emphasis added) (KJV)

Here the devil basically told them that they could create their own morality and choose their own paths. For them, God was not needed. This move, as we know, resulted in their banishment from the garden. Every single problem in the face of the earth today can be traced back to that moment.

> *How art thou fallen from heaven, O Lucifer, son of the morning! how art thou cut down to the ground, which didst weaken the nations!*
>
> *For thou hast said in thine heart, I will ascend into heaven, I will exalt my throne above the stars of God: I will sit also upon the mount of the congregation, in the sides of the north:*

I will ascend above the heights of the clouds; I will be like the most High.

Yet thou shalt be brought down to hell, to the sides of the pit.

- Isaiah 14:12-15 (KJV)

The desire in the human heart to be as God originated with Lucifer – who is now known as satan. For this sin, he was kicked out of heaven. Therefore all these impulses come from the devil. It is a demonic thing for any man to claim that he is a god.

Thus saith the Lord the King of Israel, and his redeemer the Lord of hosts; I am the first, and I am the last; and beside me there is no God.

And who, as I, shall call, and shall declare it, and set it in order for me, since I appointed the ancient people? and the things that are coming, and shall come, let them shew unto them.

Fear ye not, neither be afraid: have not I told thee from that time, and have declared it? ye are even my witnesses. Is there a God beside me? yea, there is no God; I know not any.

- Isaiah 44:6-8 (KJV)

Here God states His case very plainly: there is no God but He and if there are they are challenged to step forward and reveal themselves to Him. Here He makes it clear that there is no other God. In Isaiah 44-45 He reports this theme over and over again. By trying to become like God, one is acting like Lucifer, which if not repented of and renounced will result in the same condemnation.

Ye are my witnesses, saith the Lord, and my servant whom I have chosen: that ye may know and believe me, and understand that I am he: before me there was no God formed, neither shall there be after me.

- Isaiah 43:10 (KJV)

Mormonism teaches that there are many gods over many

worlds. Isaiah 43:10 shows that there was no God before Yahweh, He is the first – an apparent contradiction of the teachings of Mormonism.

> God is not a man, that he should lie; neither the son of man, that he should repent: hath he said, and shall he not do it? or hath he spoken, and shall he not make it good?
>
> > *- Numbers 23:19 (KJV)*

This destroys the notion that God is a man like us.

> For there are three that bear record in heaven, the Father, the Word, and the Holy Ghost: and these three are one.
>
> > *- 1 John 5:7 (KJV)*

This makes it clear that there is not three distinct gods but rather One God in three Persons. The Word is Jesus (*See John 1:1 & Revelation 19:13*).

Answering The Issa Of Islam

It is believed by Muslims that the Prophet in Deuteronomy 18:18-19 whom God would raise up among the brethren of the Israelites was Muhammad because the Israelites were their brethren whom Muhammad came from.[2] But this is not true. God does not consider the Ishmaelites the Israelites brothers (maybe cousins because of Isaac and Ishmael). Instead, if any nation of people can be regarded as the brethren of the Israelites, it was Edom. The Ishmaelites are not referred to as the brother or brethren of the Israelite, as shown in the following Scriptures:

> Obil the Ishmaelite had charge of the camels; and Jehdeiah the Meronothite had charge of the donkeys.
>
> > *- 1 Chronicles 27:30*

> Yet Gideon said to them, "I would request of you, that each of you give me an earring from his spoil." (For they had gold earrings,

because they were Ishmaelites.)

- Judges 8:24

For they have conspired together with one mind;
Against You they make a covenant:
The tents of Edom and the Ishmaelites,
Moab and the Hagrites;
Gebal and Ammon and Amalek,
Philistia with the inhabitants of Tyre;
Assyria also has joined with them;
They have become a help to the children of Lot.

- Psalm 83:5-8

By contrast, the following Scriptures show that Edom qualifies as the brother of Israel:

*From Kadesh Moses then sent messengers **to the king of Edom:** **"Thus your brother Israel has said,** 'You know all the hardship that has befallen us.*

- Numbers 20:14 (Emphasis added)

"You shall not detest an Edomite, for he is your brother; you shall not detest an Egyptian, because you were an alien in his land.

- Deuteronomy 23:7

and Esau said to Jacob, "Please let me have a swallow of that red stuff there, for I am famished." Therefore his name was called Edom.

- Genesis 25:30

Now these are the records of the generations of Esau (that is, Edom)... So Esau lived in the hill country of Seir; Esau is Edom.

- Genesis 36:1,8

These passages of Scriptures show that Edom, Jacob's (i.e. Israel's [Genesis 32:28]) brother. Besides this repeatedly Deuteronomy refers to the Israelites being each other's brothers. The Man, therefore, that God would raise up would be a Hebrew man – this is Jesus Christ. And He is more than just a prophet.

In the beginning was the Word, and the Word was with God, and the Word was God. He was in the beginning with God.

- John 1 :1-2

And the Word became flesh, and dwelt among us, and we saw His glory, glory as of the only begotten from the Father, full of grace and truth.

- John 1:14

Here it is seen that Jesus was God in the beginning. The Bible does not leave room for other opinions concerning His identity.

who, although He existed in the form of God, did not regard equality with God a thing to be grasped, but emptied Himself, taking the form of a bond-servant, and being made in the likeness of men.

- Philippians 2:6-7

At the beginning, He was God yet took on Himself the form of a Man, this in Christianity is called the Incarnation.

For in Him all the fullness of Deity dwells in bodily form.

- Colossians 2:9

The teaching of Jesus was not the same as every other prophet given before Him:

Truly, truly, I say to you, he who believes has eternal life. I am the bread of life. Your fathers ate the manna in the wilderness, and they died. This is the bread which comes down out of heaven, so that one may eat of it and not die. I am the living bread that came down out of heaven; if anyone eats of this bread, he will live forever; and the bread also which I will give for the life of the world is My flesh."

- John 6:47-51

Now on the last day, the great day of the feast, Jesus stood and cried out, saying, "If anyone is thirsty, let him come to Me and drink. He who believes in Me, as the Scripture said, 'From his innermost being will flow rivers of living water.'" But this He spoke of the Spirit, whom those who believed in Him were to receive; for the Spirit was not yet given, because Jesus was not yet glorified.

- John 7:37-39

Jesus Christ is pointing to Himself, not to another messenger who was to come (Muhammad). As for this belief held by Muslims that Jesus never said He was God or the Son of God:[3]

*Your father Abraham rejoiced to see My day, and he saw it and was glad." So the Jews said to Him, "You are not yet fifty years old, and have You seen Abraham?" Jesus said to them, **"Truly, truly, I say to you, before Abraham was born, I am."** Therefore they picked up stones to throw at Him, but Jesus hid Himself and went out of the temple.*

- John 8:56-59 (Emphasis added)

Jesus is making it very clear here that not just a mere prophet but God Himself. The Jews picked up on this and were going to stone Him. He refers to Himself as I AM, an obvious reference to Exodus 3:14 where God reveals Himself to Moses as 'I AM WHO I AM.' He also does declare Himself to be the Son of God:

I and the Father are one."

*The Jews picked up stones again to stone Him. Jesus answered them, "I showed you many good works from the Father; for which of them are you stoning Me?" The Jews answered Him, "For a good work we do not stone You, but for blasphemy; and **because You, being a man, make Yourself out to be God."** Jesus answered them, "Has it not been written in your Law, 'I said, you* *are gods'? If he called them gods, to whom the word of God came (and the Scripture cannot be broken),* **do you say of Him, whom the Father sanctified and sent into the world,** *'You are blaspheming,'* **because I said, 'I am the Son of God'***?*

- John 10:30-36 (Emphasis added)

The high priest stood up and came forward and questioned Jesus, saying, "Do You not answer? What is it that these men are testifying against You?" But He kept silent and did not answer. Again the high priest was questioning Him, and saying to Him, **"Are You the Christ, the Son of the Blessed One?" And Jesus said, "I am;** *and you shall see the Son of Man sitting at the right hand of Power, and coming with the clouds of heaven."*

- Mark 14:60-62 (Emphasis added)

He said to them, "But who do you say that I am?" Simon Peter answered, "You are the Christ, the Son of the living God." And Jesus said to him, "Blessed are you, Simon Barjona, because flesh and blood did not reveal this to you, but My Father who is in heaven.

- Matthew 16:15-17

Jesus never rebuked Peter for calling Him the Son of God thereby affirming Peter's statement. Not to mention the times that Jesus Christ accepted worship (*See Matthew 14:33, Matthew 28:9, Luke 24:52 & John 9:38*).

The angel Gabriel is not the Holy Spirit but a messenger of God. The Holy Spirit is promised to all believers (*See Romans 8:11*), and it is impossible for an angel to be in more than one place at a time for they are finite creatures.

Answering The Catholic Jesus

There is much to be said about the teaching of purgatory. Simply put: The Bible does not support such a view.

but if we walk in the Light as He Himself is in the Light, we have

*fellowship with one another, **and the blood of Jesus His Son***
***cleanses us from all sin**. If we say that we have no sin, we are*
deceiving ourselves and the truth is not in us. If we confess our
sins, He is faithful and righteous to forgive us our sins and to
cleanse us from all unrighteousness.

- 1 John 1:7-9 (Emphasis added)

Notice the word 'all.' He cleanses from **all** sin. He cleanses from **all** unrighteousness. When He died on the cross, He paid the price – **once for all** (*See Hebrews 7:27, Hebrews 9:12 & Hebrews 10:10!*). If you think this is not the case, then it is your pride in your good deeds thinking that they help Jesus' blood where it lacks. This is unthinkable and unbiblical.

Now when the Bible talks about confession here, it is not talking about confession to a priest. Many confess their sins to a priest to receive forgiveness but have no intention of stopping their evil deeds. This is to do with confessing sins to God to forsake them. James 5 speaks about us confessing our sins to one another for reconciliation, accountability, etc. But to receive forgiveness from God, it should be God alone that one confesses the sin to.

And we indeed are suffering justly, for we are receiving what we
deserve for our deeds; but this man has done nothing wrong."
And he was saying, "Jesus, remember me when You come in Your
*kingdom!" And He said to him, "**Truly I say to you, today you***
***shall be with Me in Paradise.**"*

- Luke 23:41-43 (Emphasis added)

The thief was repentant and had a change of heart. He had no time to pile up good deeds. It was 'today' that Jesus promised him paradise, the very same day he died. Absence of confession, lack of the sinner's prayer, absence of baptism and by the skin of his teeth he made it. He cried to Jesus for mercy and received it.

And inasmuch as it is appointed for men to die once and after
this comes judgment, so Christ also, having been offered once to
bear the sins of many, will appear a second time for salvation

without reference to sin, to those who eagerly await Him.

- Hebrews 9:27-28

Judgment is cast on where to go after you die – heaven or hell. So then the decision comes straight away. There is no purgatory holding cell as the choice is already firmly made and settled. The born-again person goes to be with the Lord immediately on death, and God's enemies will suffer punishment while awaiting that final judgment (see 2 Peter 2:9). That the sentence they will suffer (*while awaiting the final judgment*) is frequently not in this life is evident from, for example, Psalm 73 and Luke 16:25 (*the rich and Lazarus*). There is undoubtedly no purgatory (which is supposed as a place of improvement in preparation for heaven), but the great white throne judgement will be a right judgment of all the dead who weren't already raised in the first resurrection.

It is thought that by giving money to the Church, a soul is released from Purgatory.[4]

> *For thus says the Lord, "You were sold for nothing and you will be redeemed without money."*
>
> *- Isaiah 52:3*

> *Even those who trust in their wealth*
> *And boast in the abundance of their riches?*
> *No man can by any means redeem his brother*
> *Or give to God a ransom for him—*
> *For the redemption of his soul is costly,*
> *And he should cease trying forever—*
> *That he should live on eternally,*
> *That he should not undergo decay.*
>
> *- Psalm 49:6-9*

Money cannot be used to gain entrance to heaven. Simon the sorcerer, tried to buy the gift of the laying of hands to give the Holy Spirit. Peter's response to him tells us everything we need to know:

But Peter said to him, "May your silver perish with you, because you thought you could obtain the gift of God with money! You have no part or portion in this matter, for your heart is not right before God. Therefore repent of this wickedness of yours, and pray the Lord that, if possible, the intention of your heart may be forgiven you.

- Acts 8:20

Neither God nor His gifts can be bought with money.

Those who buy them slay them and go unpunished, and each of those who sell them says, 'Blessed be the Lord, for I have become rich!' And their own shepherds have no pity on them.

- Zechariah 11:5

These are the so-called leaders in the Church, the priests or pastors. These are those who get rich off the backs of those whom they are supposed to be looking after. They rob them of their money while denying them the truth. God will hold them responsible for their souls. God is not interested in money because He would much rather have your hearts. That is why the thief on the cross made it, at the last minute, he finally came to his senses.

"Ho! Every one who thirsts, come to the waters;
And you who have no money come, buy and eat.
Come, buy wine and milk
Without money and without cost.

- Isaiah 55:1

It also says a few verses onwards:

Seek the Lord while He may be found;
Call upon Him while He is near.
Let the wicked forsake his way
And the unrighteous man his thoughts;
And let him return to the Lord,
And He will have compassion on him,

And to our God,
For He will abundantly pardon.

- Isaiah 55:6-7

Now the attention shall be turned to Mary and her role in Christianity. The idea that she should be sinless is entirely inconceivable. This flies in the face of scripture:

as it is written,

"There is none righteous, not even one;
There is none who understands,
There is none who seeks for God;
All have turned aside, together they have become useless;
There is none who does good,
There is not even one."
"Their throat is an open grave,
With their tongues they keep deceiving,"
"The poison of asps is under their lips";

- Romans 3:10-13

Mary did not ascend into heaven, for such an account can never be found in Scripture. There is only one Person who has ascended:

No one has ascended into heaven, but He who descended from heaven: the Son of Man.

- John 3:13

Therefore it says,

"When He ascended on high,
He led captive a host of captives,
And He gave gifts to men."

(Now this expression, "He ascended," what does it mean except that He also had descended into the lower parts of the earth? He who descended is Himself also He who ascended far above all the

heavens, so that He might fill all things.)

- Ephesians 4:8-10

Mary is not even our mother. The heavenly Jerusalem is:

Now this Hagar is Mount Sinai in Arabia and corresponds to the present Jerusalem, for she is in slavery with her children. But the Jerusalem above is free; she is our mother.

- Galatians 4:25-26

She is not the mother of God, for God, the Son existed eternally before she was born. She was the mother of Jesus the Man, and only as Man. She is indeed called blessed (*Luke 1:41-48*) but must not be considered as an intermediary for us (*1 Timothy 2:5*). The idea of a Queen over all things including heaven comes from Babylon and is actually related to the goddess Ishtar (*See Jeremiah 44:15-19*). So Catholicism is a blend of Christianity and the Babylonian religion with Mary as Christianised Ishtar or Astarte and Jesus as a Christianised Baal. So therefore, the origin of this idea is not Christian but pagan. And it must be approached as such.

There are many sincere Christians who vehemently declare that Catholics are true Christians because they believe the same as Christians about Jesus. Now, while this may be true to an extent, as you have just read, there are other beliefs that they hold to that are certainly not the same, particularly the reverence and awe for Mary. If they hold to these teachings, then you as a Christian can get as mad at me as you like for saying it, but they are not part of the true Church. This is the truth, wherever you like it or not. If they were to read the Bible then they would not find any of their teachings in it, but sadly many Catholics do not read the Bible but take ideas and beliefs from their priest and the pope (*sadly the same goes for many evangelicals today who lean on the Pastor, they will hear the dreaded words of Matthew 7:23*). The true Church finds her comfort in Christ, not in Mary, any other person, thing or religious act.

What Is The Common Denominator Between These Religions?

For a start, they all claim a belief in the Bible, yet it is believed by Mormons, JWs and Muslims that the Bible is corrupt. But that is the only place where their agreements stay. And this is because they have their own teachings and holy books that contradict the Bible (so saying that the Bible is corrupt is a convenient explanation for these discrepancies). They contend that they believe in Jesus Christ, but what is the one thing that binds them all together?

The answer is that they are all a religion of works, doing good to build up a credit of righteousness before God. For Muslims it is keeping the five pillars of Islam, for Mormons it is to prove one's worth to the heavenly father – (*for we know that it is by grace that we are saved, after all we can do – 2 Nephi 25:23*), [5] for JWs it is by faith in Jehovah's baptism, *"provided... they abide in him, keeping their conscience through faith and loyal service,"*[6] and for the Catholics it is about good works, keeping the tradition of the church and obeying the authority of the clergy.

Yet in light of all of this, what does Scripture say? Can a man get to heaven through good deeds and religious devotion as he strives in himself to be and do good?

> *Therefore, just as through one man sin entered into the world, and death through sin, and so death spread to all men, because all sinned.*

> *- Romans 5:12*

It does not matter how big or small the sin is the fact remains it still brings death – for everybody. Not one person is exempt. Since one is already spiritually dead, no amount of good is useful. Good deeds do not bring dead people out of graves! Spiritually it is the same principle.

For all of us have become like one who is unclean,
And all our righteous deeds are like a filthy garment;
And all of us wither like a leaf,
And our iniquities, like the wind, take us away.

- Isaiah 64:6

This presents humanity with a huge problem. God cannot stand sin because He is holy. No sin. Not even a trace. When Jesus went to the cross, all the anger and hatred of God against sin fell on Him. He took the punishment for sin. This is because He lived that perfect and sinless life that God absolutely requires so that He was able to be a substitute. By putting faith in Christ and repenting of sin, we are acquitted from sin and are therefore brought into a right relationship with God. Good acts are to be built on top of that foundation, but they are not the foundation of themselves or grounds for God to accept us (*Please see 1 Corinthians 3:9-15 & Ephesians 2:10*).

He made Him who knew no sin to be sin on our behalf, so that we might become the righteousness of God in Him.

- 2 Corinthians 5:21

No one can earn enough credit to be saved from the wrath of God.

For by grace you have been saved through faith; and that not of yourselves, it is the gift of God; not as a result of works, so that no one may boast.

- Ephesians 2:8-9

For Jesus, salvation and entrance to heaven is so simple:

And Moses made a bronze serpent and set it on the standard; and it came about, that if a serpent bit any man, when he looked to the bronze serpent, he lived.

- Numbers 21:9

As Moses lifted up the serpent in the wilderness, even so must the

Son of Man be lifted up; so that whoever believes will in Him have eternal life.

"For God so loved the world, that He gave His only begotten Son, that whoever believes in Him shall not perish, but have eternal life.

- John 3:14-16

The message of the real Jesus is simply this: ***LOOK AND LIVE!***

In other words, look to Jesus Christ crucified and risen from the dead, and you will receive eternal life!

CHAPTER ELEVEN: THE PROBLEM OF APPROVAL

Part of the problem with today's Christians is something that affects everybody in some shape or form, it is a problem among young women, but men face it as well. It is a problem of identity. Many Christians struggle with deep-rooted insecurity in who they are. They don't even know who they are, and this creates a big problem. All people need to feel belonged and part of a group:

> ***God sets the lonely in families,***
> *he leads out the prisoners with singing;*
> *but the rebellious live in a sun-scorched land.*
>
> *- Psalm 68:6 (Emphasis added) (NIV)*

It is by God's design that each human being should be a part of a family. The Church is to be a family of all those who believe in Christ.

> *Show proper respect to everyone, **love the family of believers**,*
> *fear God, honor the emperor.*
>
> *- 1 Peter 2:17 (Emphasis added) (NIV)*

The problem is that because many Christians don't understand their value and worth in God's eyes, they turn to people for approval and support. Christians lean on people, even people of the world because of deep-rooted insecurities. There are many factors in situations like these, but the root cause is due to rejection. Either from a significant figure like a parent or a role model, or a peer from bullying or separation. They look for approval from other people because they don't approve of themselves.

> *to the praise of the glory of His grace, by which He made us accepted in the Beloved.*
>
> *- Ephesians 1:6 (NKJV)*

Every Christian is accepted in the Beloved. Every believer is greatly valued by God. Every tear shed and every drop of blood belonging to a Christian is precious in the eyes of God:

> *You have taken account of my wanderings;*
> *Put my tears in Your bottle.*
> *Are they not in Your book?*
>
> *- Psalm 56:8*

> *He will rescue their life from oppression and violence,*
> *And their blood will be precious in his sight;*
>
> *- Psalm 72:14*

Yet why is there this crippling identity problem? The answer is straightforward. Christians don't really believe that God loves them. They can understand it for other people sure, and they can know that the Bible tells them that God loves them, but they have a hard time believing it for themselves.

God is calling these people back into a love relationship with Him. If this is you, you must understand how precious you are in the eyes of God. He loves you so much that He sent His own Son to be crucified for you to come into a right relationship with Him. If you were the only person on the face of the earth, God still would have sent Jesus to die, just for you.

We have come to know and have believed the love which God has for us. God is love, and the one who abides in love abides in God, and God abides in him.

- 1 John 4:16

If you are a lonely person, Jesus Christ wants to draw near to you in your loneliness. For every soul is yearning for love and relationship that can only come from God. You don't have to be lonely anymore; your identity needs to be found in Jesus Christ alone. When you die, and He lives – that is when you will have found who you really are.

In my life, I studied Performing Arts with the hope of becoming an Actor. Although I thought I did it because I enjoyed it the real reason was that I was deeply insecure in my identity and sought to become another person when I acted. I became a Christian and gave up acting, yet I still had terribly deep insecurities and a longing for acceptance among people. Even though I prayed a lot, and read the Bible as I enjoyed fellowship with God, I felt far from God at large. I understood His holiness and righteousness. Even though I was a Christian and God had made peace with me, I just couldn't understand how a holy, pure and righteous God could ever love such a wretched sinner like me. How was it possible that such a good God could love a lousy person like me? Even in one point during my time at Bible College, I heard the Holy Spirit speak to my heart, I think with tears, he said:

"I approve of you, why don't you approve of yourself?"

I found my identity when I stopped putting my hope in people. I gave up caring what people thought of me because the Lord taught me not to rely on fallible human beings but to lean only, totally and completely on Him. He wants to do the same with you!

For you have died and your life is hidden with Christ in God.

- Colossians 3:3

As you give your life to Jesus Christ, your identity is no longer based on you and who you are, but it is wholly found in Him! When a woman gets married here in the UK, she loses her old name and receives a new name – the name of her husband. When you become a Christian, you lose your old name: Sinner. You gain a new Name: in Christ, or Christian. He puts His Name on You!

So that the rest of mankind may seek the Lord,
And all the Gentiles who are called by My name,'

- Acts 15:17

Do they not blaspheme the fair name by which you have been called?

-James 2:7

The world cannot comfort you, and other Christians cannot give you the identity you long for. The world cannot give you the approval that you need. That can only come from God. Leave the world and the cares, thoughts and opinions of people who are only here for a temporal time. Seek your approval from the eternal God!

He who overcomes, I will make him a pillar in the temple of My
God, and he will not go out from it anymore; and I will write on
him the name of My God, and the name of the city of My God, the
new Jerusalem, which comes down out of heaven from My God,
and My new name.

- Revelation 3:12

CHAPTER TWELVE:
CHEAP GRACE

T he Gospel of Jesus Christ is the only thing in this world that
has supreme value over all things. And it is because of this
Gospel that many have laid down their lives.

Then I heard a loud voice in heaven, saying,

*"Now the salvation, and the power, and the kingdom of our God
and the authority of His Christ have come, for the accuser of our
brethren has been thrown down, he who accuses them before our
God day and night. And they overcame him because of the blood
of the Lamb and because of the word of their testimony, **and
they did not love their life even when faced with death.***

- Revelation 12:13 (Emphasis added)

This is the heart of every true believer, they do not hold to
their lives so tightly as to shrink back in the face of dying for
the faith. In the Western world the Gospel of Jesus Christ has
been cheapened in many churches. Though there are many faithful God-fearing, Christ-loving churches, for not all churches are
cheapening the Gospel. And it's not that the Gospel can really be
cheapened but rather has been substituted for another gospel. In
one church, for a Christmas appeal, everyone received a card with
a silly little Christmas greeting. There was nothing to do with the
Gospel on it. There was also a blank space was for any would be

converts to write their names on and bring it to the front. That was their coming to Christ. Many non-Christians attended this Christmas service. There was no clear gospel presentation, a brief mention of the cross, with people mostly talking about the first-ever Christmas party. Understandably, Christmas is to be a joyful time, but one must understand why it is a joyful occasion! It is so because God came into the world to redeem mankind from sin and hell. Not so that people can party and dance around, having a good time.

Many, if not all, lost people don't want a relationship with God; they want to have their pleasure and sins. Therefore, a church that doesn't challenge them or call them to repentance, but rather, caters to their sinful craving is perfect for them, in their eyes. These churches are very popular, and this is the reason.

"An appalling and horrible thing
Has happened in the land:
The prophets prophesy falsely,
And the priests rule on their own authority;
And My people love it so!
But what will you do at the end of it?

- Jeremiah 5:30-31

If you were to speak out about this, for sure someone would tell you that you were to see the good in what they are doing and how successful they are. It seems that the majority of people see these modern churches and believe them to be successful because they have many people in attendance, with a big budget as a result of the huge inflow of money they receive. But that is not how God rates success.

A young girl attending one of these identified herself as Christian to me. Yet she practised sexual immorality with no thought of it as being evil. She also affirmed homosexuality as being perfectly acceptable. By her life, and her views, she contradicted what God revealed in His Word. And all the while, holding on to the title of Christian.

At the same time there was a man who has been attending a church for nine years, he was baptised and thought nothing of living with his girlfriend. He even expressed belief that there is no hell and that everyone will find God eventually.

So what happened there? What went wrong? It's obvious. You have lost people coming to church and becoming religious (while remaining lost). They claim to love God but they hold onto their sins. They never come to the place that the love for God is supposed to take them.

> *always learning and never able to come to the knowledge of the truth.*
>
> *- 2 Timothy 3:7*

Why does this sort of thing go on? Why is it so rife today? The main reason for this is because many people who preach or teach in the pulpits today are cowards. Not all preachers or teachers I must add. There are many great Bible teachers and preachers today who stand up as God's men, but they are far outnumbered by those who preach lies.

The ones who speak falsehood care more about the size of the church than the condition of it. They care more about getting people into the building than getting lost souls into heaven. They therefore do not preach or teach what God would have them (then otherwise these people might leave their church taking their money with them) but rather what everybody wants to hear. All about how much they are loved by God and how Jesus wants to be their best friend. Even while these same people live in sin, and that is never spoken about let alone ever challenged. They therefore go to church and think they deserve to go to heaven because of their religiousness or supposed goodness, when in fact they are children of the devil (*Please see 1 John 3:10!*) and are going to die and go to hell. And all of this is because they are not being told that they must repent of their sins and be born again.

Shame on those preachers! They send people to hell so that they can keep their positions in the church. The grace of the Lord Jesus Christ is indeed free but it is by no means cheap. It cost God the death of His only begotten Son. Such a heavy price! And what conditions did Jesus place on anyone who would follow Him?

"If anyone comes to Me, and does not hate his own father and mother and wife and children and brothers and sisters, yes, and even his own life, he cannot be My disciple. Whoever does not carry his own cross and come after Me cannot be My disciple.

- Luke 14:26-27

What a cost! Do you see that? This is not a cheap, frivolous, sign your name on a card, salvation. No! Jesus Christ never offers such a salvation! For God puts His Name on those that come to Him and He will by no means allow His holy Name to be trampled on. The intended message by Jesus is a hyperbole, for your devotion to Him must trump your devotion even to your parents. You must also be willing to completely die to yourself. Giving up all your personal ambitions and living alone for God. Yet a few verses later Jesus had the following to say:

So then, none of you can be My disciple who does not give up all his own possessions.

- Luke 14:33

This is the complete opposite of what many churches say today with all this prosperity poo. Much of it is lies, intended to make people feel good. But people who are in sin don't need to feel good they need to learn to feel godly sorrow!

"Blessed are those who mourn, for they shall be comforted.

- Matthew 5:4

Only the mourners receive the comfort, those who mourn over their sin and inner wretchedness. The comfort of Christ is never given to anyone who refuses to depart from their evil.

Afterwards there can be joy in the Holy Spirit but that joy comes out of repentance. It comes from a life of obedience to God, it is not an automatic joy that comes because you verbally affirm a creed or believe in the existence of a God (*See James 2:19*).

> *I now rejoice, not that you were made sorrowful, but that you were made sorrowful to the point of repentance; for you were made sorrowful according to the will of God, so that you might not suffer loss in anything through us. For the sorrow that is according to the will of God produces a repentance without regret, leading to salvation, but the sorrow of the world produces death.*
>
> *- 2 Corinthians 7:9-10*

God wants His people to march only for the Kingdom of God and to stop playing religious games like little boys. It's time to be men! So, man up.

> *Suffer hardship with me, as a good soldier of Christ Jesus. No soldier in active service entangles himself in the affairs of everyday life, so that he may please the one who enlisted him as a soldier.*
>
> *- 2 Timothy 2:3-4*

REFERENCES

Epigraph

Quote retrieved from: https://www.goodreads.com/author/quotes/159020.Leonard_Ravenhill

Chapter Three: Internet – The New Babel?

[1]https://www.huffingtonpost.co.uk/2013/05/03/internet-porn-stats_n_3187682.html
[2]Ibid.
[3]www.expastors.com/how-many-pastors-are-addicted-to-porn-the-stats-are-surprising/

Chapter Four: The Enemy Within

[1]*Heart Publications*, August/September 2018 issue
[2]https://www.bbc.co.uk/news/uk-37269471
[3]https://www.dailymail.co.uk/news/article-2963449/Vital-breakthrough-scientists-playing-God-Church-leader-no-doubt-says-MUST-T-let-flat-earthers-stand-way-three-parent-babies.html
[4]*Heart Publications*, August/September 2018 issue
[5]Some ideas taken from David Wilkerson, A. A. SermonIndex.net. (2016, December 15). Audio Sermon: Falling Away to the Anti christ by David Wilkerson. Retrieved from https://www.you-tube.com/watch?v=UES7Ct5zhds
[6]Some ideas taken from Derek Prince, A. A. Powerful Preaching and Teaching. (2019, April). 4242 - Derek Prince - Witchcraft

Exposed And Defeated - Witchcraft Unveiled. Retrieved from https://www.youtube.com/watch?v=N9EPlILVrAg

Chapter Five: Despising The Word

[1]https://en.oxforddictionaries.com/definition/relativism

Chapter Six: Apathy – The Killer Of Christian Passion

[1]*The Pilgrim's Progress from This World to That Which Is to Come*, John Bunyan, 1678
[2]David Wilkerson, The Cost of a Fresh Anointing, The Hope That Purifies Minister's Conference, 2007

Chapter Seven: The Deceptive Power Of Feelings

[1]The New Strong's Expanded Exhaustive Concordance of the Bible, Red Letter Edition, Thomas Nelson Publishers, 2001, G1228

Chapter Eight: Holiness – The Evangelical Elephant In The Room

[1]The New Strong's Expanded Exhaustive Concordance of the Bible, Red Letter Edition, Thomas Nelson Publishers, 2001, G37
[2]The New Strong's Expanded Exhaustive Concordance of the Bible, Red Letter Edition, Thomas Nelson Publishers, 2001, G3700

Chapter Nine: The Many False Faces Of Jesus – Part One

[1]Keith Green, A. A. Myke A. (2016, December 27). Keith Green 1982 100 Huntley Street TV 01 Keith's Testimony. Retrieved from https://www.youtube.com/watch?v=oOYQSn46q08

[2]*New World Translation of the Holy Scriptures*, WATCHTOWER BIBLE AND TRACT SOCIETY OF NEW YORK INC. Wallkill, New York, U.S.A. 2003

[3]Ibid.

[4]*What Does the Bible Really Teach?*, Watchtower Bible and Tract Society of New York, Inc. Brooklyn, New York, U.S.A. December 2014 Printing

[5]Ibid.

[6]Ibid.

[7]Jeremiah Films, A. A. Jeremiah Films (2011, May 27). Banned Mormon Cartoon - EXTENDED VERSION. Retrieved from https://www.youtube.com/watch?v=n3BqLZ8UoZk

[8]Ibid.

[9]https://www.lds.org/manual/jesus-the-christ/chapter-2?lang=eng

[10]https://www.whyislam.org/common-ground/Muhammad-a-prophet-like-unto-moses/

[11]https://www.catholic.com/tract/scripture-and-tradition

[12]http://archeparchy.ca/wcm-docs/docs/catechism-of-the-catholic-church.pdf

[13]Ibid.

[14]Ibid.

[15]Ibid.

[16]Some books I can recommend for further reading are: *Comparing Christianity with the CULTS* by Keith L. Brooks, Irvine Robertson & Dillon Burroughs, *Debate* by Reinaldo de Melo, *The Mosque* by Belteshazzar & Abednego and *Not the Same God* by Sam Solomon. I also recommend the link: https://www.youtube.com/watch?v=n3BqLZ8UoZk for more information concerning Mormonism.

Chapter Ten: The Many False Faces Of Jesus – Part Two

[1]*The New Strong's Expanded Exhaustive Concordance of the Bible*, Red Letter Edition, Thomas Nelson Publishers, 2001

[2]https://www.whyislam.org/common-ground/Muhammad-a-

prophet-like-unto-moses/

[3]Dr Zakir Naik, A. A. Dr Zakir Naik. (2014, November 12). "Jesus Christ (pbuh) never claimed that he is God" - Dr Zakir Naik. Retrieved from https://www.youtube.com/watch?v=u3Z-XFq8F_w&pbjreload=10

[4]https://forums.catholic.com/t/paying-for-souls-in-purgatory/408441

[5]*The Book of Mormon – Another Testament of Jesus Christ*, The Church of Latter-day Saints, Salt Lake City, Utah, USA, 1981, 2013 by Intellectual Reserve, Inc.

[6]Keith L. Brooks, Irvine Robertson & Dillon Burroughs, *Comparing Christianity with the CULTS*, The Moody Bible Institute of Chicago, Fourth revised edition, 1969, 1975, 1976, 1985, 2007

ACKNOWLEDGEMENT

Writing this book was hard work, and it entailed a lot of research. Yet, it would not have been possible without the input of a few others. I want to thank Malcolm Leicester-Smith and Gideon Onumah for being among those who read through and gave some interesting comments.

Thank you, Frank Cook, for giving me a very good concise theological polish to this book. I also want to thank Bethany Hastings for helping me to season my book with a bit more grace and gentleness when I came across as too harsh or overbearing. I also want to thank Stephen Brunton for reading this book and giving a lot of encouragement to keep going in my walk with the Lord.

I also want to thank my friends Lena Parle and Gessica Tiberio for being my lovely test readers and encouraging me.

My biggest gratitude is for my Saviour, Jesus Christ. My Lord. Who has demonstrated to me infinite patience in bringing me out of my own Babylon and continues to deal gently with me concerning the compromises in my life.

> *May the lamb that was slain receive the full reward of His suffering!*

Printed in Poland
by Amazon Fulfillment
Poland Sp. z o.o., Wrocław